Augsburg College
George Sverdrup Library
Minneapolis, MN 55454

THE DIFFICULT BORDER:

CURRENT RUSSIAN AND CHINESE CONCEPTS OF SINO-RUSSIAN RELATIONS AND FRONTIER PROBLEMS

THE DIFFICULT BORDER:

CURRENT RUSSIAN AND CHINESE CONCEPTS OF SINO-RUSSIAN RELATIONS AND FRONTIER PROBLEMS

Alexei D. Voskressenski

Nova Science Publishers, Inc.
New York

Art Director: Maria Ester Hawrys
Assistant Director: Elenor Kallberg
Graphics: Denise Dieterich and Kerri Pfister
Manuscript Coordinator: Roseann Pena
Book Production: Tammy Sauter, Benjamin Fung
Circulation: Irene Kwartiroff and Annette Hellinger

Library of Congress Cataloging-in-Publication Data

Voskressenski, Alexei D.
    The difficult border : current Russian and Chinese concepts of Sino-Russian relations and frontier problems / Alexei D. Voskressenski.
      p. cm.
    Includes bibliographical references and index.
    ISBN 1-56072-207-6 : $69
    1. Russia (Federation)—Foreign relations—China. 2. China—Foreign relations—Russia (Federation). 3. Russia (Federation)—Boundaries—China. 4. China—Boundaries—Russia (Federation). I. Title.
DK68.7.C6V67   1995
327.47051—dc20   94-41592
                                                                                 CIP

Copyright © 1996 by Nova Science Publishers, Inc.
                    6080 Jericho Turnpike, Suite 207
                    Commack, New York 11725
                    Tele. 516-499-3103 Fax 516-499-3146
                    E Mail Novascil@aol.com

All rights reserved. No part of this book may be reproduced, stored in a retrieval system or transmitted in any form or by any means: electronic, electrostatic, magnetic, tape, mechanical photocopying, recording or otherwise without permission from the publishers

Printed in the United States of America

Contents

Acknowledgment v
I. Introduction 1
II. Organization of Studies on Sino-Russian Relations
 in Russia and China 9
III. The Problem of Sources 11
V. Chinese Approaches 23
 A. *General Chinese Concepts of Sino-Russian Relations
 and Border Problems* 23
 1. Dominant Paradigm 23
 2. Attitudes Toward Imperial Russia 27
 3. National Histories 28
 4. New Chinese Scholarship 38
 B. *Chinese Scholars About the History of Sino-Russian Relations
 and History of the Formation of Sino-Russian Border.* 40
 1. Sino-Russian Relations
 and Formation of the Border 40
 2. The Chinese Survey of Their Own Concepts
 and Current Conceptual Innovations 53
 3. Chinese Appraisals of Russian Concepts 61
VI. Russian Approaches 67
 A. *Russian Concepts and the Problem of 'Balanced' Interpretation
 of the Russian-Chinese Relations* 67
 1. Russian Approaches 67

    2. Creating a 'Balanced' Concept: Russian-Chinese Treaty Acts—Possible Approaches and Interpretations............70

VII. **Sino-Soviet and Sino-Russian Border Relations: From Past to Present**..87

VIII. **Conclusion**..103

IX. **Concise Chronology of Russian-Chinese Relations**......109

X. **Maps**..115A

XII. **Subject Index**..117

ACKNOWLEDGMENT

The intellectual support of the New School of Social Research (USA), mostly by Professors Eric Hobsbawm and Margaret C. Jacob, and lately by the Common Security Forum, an international group of scholars based at the University of Cambridge (UK) - Harvard University (USA) was important for my writings. A scholarship from Maison de Sciences de l'Homme (Paris, France) gave me the opportunity to discuss related problems with the French Academic community. The University of Maryland (USA), where I have been a Foreign Policy Fellow at the School of Public Affairs, became an excellent place to proceed with draft versions of this manuscript, that were prepared in part under a grant from the Kennan Institute of Advanced Russian Studies at the Woodrow Wilson International Center for Scholars, Washington, D.C. The manuscript in its current form was finished while I was in Manchester (UK).

I'm grateful to professor Vladimir S. Miasnikov, Corresponding Member of the Russian Academy of Sciences, Dr. Yevgenyi D. Stepanov (Institute of Far Eastern Studies, Russian Academy of Sciences) and Dr. Sergei N. Goncharov (Russian Foreign Ministry) for their remarks. I am equally obliged to Dr. Robert A. Gates (New School, USA), Professor Emma Rotschild (Cambridge University, UK), Dr. Flemming Christiansen (University of Manchester, UK), and Dr. Alan Hunter (University of Leeds, UK) who commented on portions of the draft, as well as to all those who discussed different parts of it at the New School, during my seminar "Chinese Historiography on Sino-Russian Relations" at the Mongolian and Inner Asian Studies Unit (King's College, Cambridge University) in October 1992, and at the Second University of Manchester Workshop on Central Asia and the Caucasus in May, 1995 I'm also grateful to Ms. Lise Grande for stylistic improvements of some sections of the text and to Mr. David A. Wallick, my assistant at the Kennan Institute, who helped me with the preparation of the manuscript, though all the inadequacies of the book are, of course, only within my own responsibility. The statements and views expressed herein are those of the author and are not necessarily those of all the above-mentioned organizations.

INTRODUCTION

The history of Sino-Russian relations and border problems as one of its most important components has long been considered a central question in the overall history of international relations in Central Asia and the Far East by Russian, Soviet,[1] and Chinese historians. Research in the field long ago ceased to be "regional" as scholars from Europe, Japan, the U.S.A., Taiwan and other countries have increasingly tried to develop their own views of the Sino-Russian relationship into a possible model for understanding both the shift in Chinese diplomatic doctrine historically, and also, a pivotal role of Russia shaping relations between China and the Western countries. The creation in 1986 of the International Association for the Study of Sino-Russian Relations has institutionalized this approach.[2]

The suicide of the Soviet Union (as Chinese political analysts call the collapse of the Soviet empire) has profoundly influenced China, insofar as events in the former Soviet Union always was and will be of crucial importance for China. Furthermore, if the fragile reforms in the former Soviet Union succeed, it is feared by the Chinese government that the people of China will also demand democracy. This would mean the end of the modern regime, the disintegration of the Chinese empire, and the emergence of a new balance of power in Asia. In addition, new separatist movements in Guangdong province are strengthening those in Tibet and Xinjiang. Though well-known in the West, the case of Tibet may be of less importance and much more local than that of Xinjiang, an autonomous region inhabited by Muslims of Turkic origin who are ethnically related to the people of the now independent states of Uzbekistan, Kyrgyzstan,

---

[1] By Soviet I mean scholars of the Soviet period.

[2] See the newsletter of the society, compiled by Mrs. Patricia Polansky, Russian Bibliographer at Hamilton Library, University of Hawaii.

Tajikistan, and Kazakhstan.³ These new, unstable states are located immediately across the former Sino-Soviet border, itself comprised of more than 30 disputed areas including that of Pamir, a region equal in territory to a large state.⁴ An armed rebellion in Xinjiang was suppressed three years ago by the Chinese authorities, yet discontent in the region continues to grow, strengthened by the success of some Central Asian nationalities in achieving independence after the collapse of the Soviet Union. China's ancient territorial disputes with its neighbors (including those in the South China Sea) and the "unsettled internal affair" with Taiwan remain sources of perturbation throughout Asia.⁵

It is common place for Chinese scholars to argue that China's weakness in the 19th-20th centuries meant that its country's leaders were unable to adequately defend the country's interests and that because of this the country has lost a considerable part of its territories traditionally considered within the "Chinese empire's sphere of influence." In terms of national psychology, this kind of loss cannot be forgotten by any great nation. However, for the first time since the collapse of the Qing empire, China is now gaining the economic and military power⁶ which could potentially constitute a basis for resolving these long-term disputes in China's favor. While the Chinese are on their way to changing their social system the process is still dubiously equal to democratization. It is quite probable that at the end of the 1990s the world will see economically more developed, yet still authoritarian China. Some political analysts believe that by the end of the century China may fill the military vacuum in the Asian-Pacific region left after the disintegration of the Soviet Union and the withdrawal of the United States from bases in the Philippines and under certain circumstances may upset the fragile balance in Asia.

The Chinese literature that I intend to analyze, though not "official" in the strict sense of representing government policy,⁷ nevertheless docu-

---

³ The custom of transliterating Central Asian names and toponyms into English from the Russianized versions is now giving way to transliteration from the Central Asian languages. I try to follow this new trend though it is not possible in all the cases.

⁴ See John W. Garver. "The Sino-Soviet Territorial Dispute in the Pamir Mauntains Region". *China Quarterly*. #85. March 1981; Ann Sheehy. "Russia and China in the Pamirs: 18th and 19th Centuries". *Central Asian Review*. Vol. 15, #1, 1968.

⁵ Nicholas D. Kristof. "China Builds Its Military Muscle, Making Some Neighbors Nervous". *The New York Times*. January 11, 1993.

⁶ "Chinese Puzzles. Developing Countries Are Less Poor than Official Figures Suggest". *The Economist*. May 15th, 1993. P. 83.

⁷ It is obvious that in a country with a highly ideological regime such as China's, nothing of strategic importance can be published without the approval of the authorities.

ments the determination of the Chinese state to recover the independent section of Mongolia, as well as those disputed strips of territory "taken" by Russia in the 19th century.[8] These territories are regarded by part of the Chinese political establishment as "lost" or "torn" from the Chinese state and therefore as a source of shame for the nation. I do not think, however, that China will try to recover these territories,[9] I simply stress the necessity of understanding the Chinese perception of these territories as a kind of periphery of the Chinese empire in view of the unprecedented changes that are currently reshaping the balance in the region.

After the collapse of the Soviet Union the newly independent Central Asian states ceased to look at Russia as a "core". Does the Russian new idea of the "responsibility" toward the former Soviet periphery mean that Russia succeeded in remaining the "core" for these states, or they are in a search of a new "core", and maybe the role of such "core" can now be taken by China, or the Muslim world?[10] The same question can be asked in view of the new trends in Russian regional development. Russia is reinventing itself, the traditional center-periphery relationship between Moscow and the Russian provinces is being transformed. Increased regional autonomy is already a reality of the Russian life. The Russian periphery has successfully extracted greater economic and political power from the central government. Will it try to find a new historical legacy to strengthen this new status? And if the answer is positive then what can be a basis for this new historical legacy?

The possible border conflict zone in Central Asia includes also a large portion of Northern Kazakhstan that is persistently claimed by the local Cossacks to be Russian. Within Central Asia itself border disputes are growing in the Osh oblast between Kyrgyz and Uzbek, in Samarkand, Bukhara and Khodzhand between Tajik and Uzbek, and in Southern Kyrgyzstan between Kyrgiz and Tajiks.[11] The roots of all these conflicts are in the history of the region.

---

[8] For a background on the Sino-Soviet territorial dispute see: David Rees. "Soviet Border Problems: China and Japan". *Conflict Studies*. Occasional Paper #139. London, Institute for the Study of Conflict, 1982; Michael J. Speltz. "Chinese Territorial Claims on the Soviet Far East". *Military Review*, Vol. 65, August 1985.

[9] For an analysis of former Soviet military considerations which in a certain sense are still valid for the Russian military see, for example, R. Menon and D. Abele. "Security Dimensions of Soviet Territorial Disputes with China and Japan". *Journal of North Asian Studies*. Vol. 8. #1, Spring 1989.

[10] Herbert M. Watzman. "7,000 Central Asian Students Enroll at Turkish Institutions". *The Chronicle of Higher Education*, June 23, 1993, Vol. XXXIX, #42, P. A29.

[11] See, James Critchlow. Central Asia's Challenge to Our Understanding. *Central Asian Monitor*. #1. 1992. P. 9-10; Igor Rotar. The Mine Set By The Kremlin's Cartographers: Border Problems Can Blow Up Central Asia. *Nezavisimaya Gazeta*. 12.25.1992.

The present weakness of Russia is obviously not beneficial to China since the partnership between Russia and the USA can only undermine China's position in the world. The "Chinese wildcard," while frequently played in the past by both the U.S.A. and the Soviet Union, is no longer as important since the end of the Cold War. While China has lost strategic importance with the collapse of the Soviet Union, as is pointed out by Nikolas Kristof,

> "... Beijing still has a dizzying capacity to disrupt the post cold-war party... Any Western oriented plan for a new international order could face major challenges from this Communist rear guard because China has nuclear warheads, three million troops and significant territorial disputes with its neighbors..."[12]

The vacuum created by the end of superpower rivalry will lead to a new balance of power in the region and perhaps, to the emergence of a new "Russian card." Considering the fact that this new balance between Russia, China and the U.S.A. will undoubtedly go far in shaping a new world order, it is important to try to anticipate the nature of this new relationship. To do this however, it is important to understand how relations between these countries developed in the past. Sino-Russian relations in general, and their border problems in particular, are one of the important parts of the international relations in Central Asia and the Far East. A recent historiography by Russian and Chinese scholars concerning these subjects provides a valuable perspective on how these two giants understand their mutual history and the history of the region. Different approaches in Russia and China toward the same historical events reflect the historical roots of instability in Central Asia and provide clues to current perceptions of Sino-Russian power struggles. It is with this in mind that the history of the region, which lays at the intersection of the interests of Russia, China and the Muslim World, and current historical concepts should be thoroughly examined. Failure of doing so can possibly lead to a situation similar to the Yugoslav quagmire but on a much larger scale.

The last ten years of Russian and Chinese historiography (1980-1990) are very important, as the historiography has inherited from the early 1980s the emergence of "open" literature[13] on Sino-Russian relations in China and the former Soviet Union. In the beginning of the 1980s (and in

---

[12] Nicolas D. Kristof. "As China Looks at World Order, It Detects New Struggles Emerging". *The New York Times*. April 21,1992.

[13] By "open" I mean the literature intended not exclusively for internal use.

the mid-1980s) in both the Soviet Union and China, attempts were being made to resolve the deadlock in Sino-Soviet relations by reinterpreting their mutual history. The beginning of the 1990s marked the end of the Soviet Union and the beginning of a new era in international relations.

Historians, specializing in Russian and Chinese studies, are familiar with the basic concepts elaborated on in Russia and China in the 1960s and 1970s mostly because the historical discussion ended by sanguinary border clashes between the two nations in the Far East and Central Asia. This was the reason for basic paradigms being analyzed in published form in Western nations.[14] The situation with current conceptual innovations is different. Because of unprecedented social changes, the historical writings in both Russia and China were neglected by the analysts. At the same time the available literature and historical concepts in most cases lag behind the social and political changes in the region, thus laying a base for potential future conflicts. In countries which lack democratic institutions or newly independent countries, a political legacy is achieved by reinterpreting the history of the region. Thus, the history in these countries becomes a part of political life and a weapon in the political struggle.

Border history and the history of relationships between neighboring countries are always very sensitive topics. This is particularly true for Russia and China. During the past decade, however the two countries have managed "to close the past and to open the future" (the words belong to Deng Xiaoping), i.e., to reject most of the ideological deformations and misunderstandings regarding their history that developed over the years. It is obvious, however, that political will is not going to be enough to resolve all the questions arising out of centuries of misinformation and mistrust. Historians in both countries still do not understand each other; their conceptual writing is developing within separate, isolated spheres of knowledge. History today in both countries -- just as it has been for hundreds of years -- is still written by the winners, and facts that do not fit within the mainstream concepts are simply rejected. Consequently the task of constructing a new, more balanced history, based on a commonly accepted body of facts, becomes urgent given the importance of strengthening mutual trust between these powerful countries.

It is necessary for the new Russian government to undertake new historical analyses of Sino-Russian border problems and their impact on the

---

[14] See, for example, *The Sino-Soviet Dispute.* Documented and analyzed by G.F. Hudson, Richard Lowental and Roderick MacFarquhar. Praeger, N.Y., 1963; D.J. Doolin. *Territorial Claims in the Sino-Soviet Border Conflict. Documents and Analyses.* Stanford University Press, 1965, 2nd ed., 1973; W.A.D. Jackson. *The Russo-Chinese Borderlands: Zone of Peaceful Contact or Potential Conflict*, 2nd ed., Princeton, N.J. Van Nostrand, 1968 etc.

international balance of power in Central Asia and the Far East, since the new government is determined to reject past imperialism and ideological dogmatism and instead to formulate a new concept of Sino-Russian relations. This kind of new formulation is dependant upon a clear understanding of how Russia's former adversaries viewed it. In addition, the new Central Asian states (former Soviet republics) and even some regions in Russia itself have all had a long history connected with the history of China. Now that their borders with China have been restored, it is very important for Russian policy-makers and the international community to understand Chinese attitudes toward those former republics and also to the Russian periphery, particularly in light of their strategic importance to Russia and China.

In this book I will try to analyze Chinese and Russian historiography of the last ten years[15] concerning the question of border relations in order to formulate a new, and more balanced interpretation of the history of Sino-Russian relations. Since the old Sino-Russian Treaties still constitute the only legal foundation of the current borders between Russia, China and the newly independent Central Asian states, this new interpretation, in turn, can hopefully become a basis for creating the conditions necessary for a more benevolent political arrangement between Russia, China and other Central Asian states. Creating the framework for the analysis of the past can help scholars and politicians to better understand the present and thus respond more sensitively for the future.

I will focus on the way problems have been posed, on the authors' ideas and the logic of their explanations, and finally on the authors' methods and their sources especially in regard to their political biases.

---

[15] Part of this literature was recently analyzed by George Ginsburgs, Professor of Law at Rutgers University in his article "Recent History of the Territorial Question in Central Asia". *Central Asia Monitor*, #2, 1992, P.31-41 (Part I); #3, P.21-29 (Part 2), though he analyzed mostly Chinese and Russian official literature of the 1970s.

ORGANIZATION OF STUDIES ON SINO-RUSSIAN RELATIONS IN CHINA AND RUSSIA

China has a very long and rich tradition of research on Russia, and has always considered it China's most important neighbor. This tradition dates back to the first years of the Qing[16] dynasty [1644-1911] when a number of central questions were raised about how to assess this powerful neighbor. These questions were further elaborated upon during the Guomindang period. Since then, different aspects of these questions have been accentuated during different periods depending upon the political situation in China; this has remained true even after the creation of the People's Republic of China.

In the last 10 years China has established a broad network of research institutions devoted to historical and contemporary problems of the former Soviet Union. Great attention has been paid to the history of Sino-Russian relations and to the history of the formation of the Sino-Russian border. Many publications have recently appeared on this issue in addition to numerous conferences and panels devoted to the theme. One of the first such conferences, and one the most important, was organized by the Association of Liaoning Province for the Study of Sino-Russian Relations together with the Center for China's Borderland History, a part of the

---

[16] I use here the Chinese pinyin transcription though it is not an American tradition to transcribe Chinese words. But even J.K.Fairbank in *The Cambridge History Of China* writes: "The Wade-Giles system ... is no doubt less-simple and efficient than the new pinyin system ...". *The Cambridge History of China*. Vol. 10. Cambridge University Press. 1988. P.XY.

All Chinese publications mentioned in the book, unless overwise specified, are in Chinese, all Russian publications are in Russian; A simplified version of references is adopted throughout the book. The Sino-Russian treaties signed before 1918 are cited by the Russian old-style calendar.

Chinese Academy of Social Sciences.[17] Since this initial conference, a number of other panels have taken up these issues, including the annual meetings of the Association of the Xinjiang historians, the Association of Beijing[18] historians, the Annual Conference on the Archives of the Ming (1368-1644) and Qing (1644-1911) dynasties, the All-China Congresses on Qing History, and the Annual Conference on the history of the formation of the Chinese frontiers. Apparently border questions are increasingly becoming part of normal scholarly life in China.

Chinese scholars' activity in this area is intense. The Chinese Academy of Social Sciences, for example, has gathered many qualified specialists in Chinese, Manchu, Mongolian, Tibetan, Russian and European languages, to work with other specialists on Russian and Chinese history. These scholars are preparing archival documents and materials for publication. Chinese publishing houses are increasingly translating and publishing in Chinese works by Russian, Western, Japanese, Taiwanese and Hong Kong scholars on the history of Sino-Russian relations. Chinese scholars are also struggling to formulate general historical principles, which are then to become the methodological basis for further study in the relevant subfields.

Most of the scholars involved in these activities are based at the Institute of History, the Institute of Modern History,[19] the Institute of Economics, the Center for the Documentation and Information of the Chinese Academy of Social Sciences and in the First Historical Archive.[20] Another specialized, independent organization is the Center for China's Borderland History.[21] This Center is responsible for the coordination of all official and scholarly research concerning the evolution of Chinese borders, history of the border policies of the Chinese authorities, the international historiography of the field, and the modern land, river and ocean frontiers of China.

Sino-Soviet and Sino-Russian relations and border problems are also being increasingly taken up in the network of provincial Academies of Social Sciences (especially those in the northern part of China). Major aca-

---

[17] I mention this conference, held in Dalian in 1986, because it was the first "open" conference in the field (the announcement and the analysis of the results of the conference were published in *Renmin Ribao*) after several decades of internal scholarly activity.

[18] I also use the old transliteration "Peking" relating to historical questions (for example, the Treaty of Peking).

[19] The leading Chinese department in the field is located here.

[20] I'm not taking into account researchers in analytical departments of the Chinese Foreign Ministry, Government bodies, various military organizations etc.

[21] Also within the system of the Academy of Social Sciences.

demic institutions in this network include: the Institute of Siberia, the Institute of History[22] at the Academy of Social Sciences of Heilongjiang province, the Institute of the History of Dongbei (known also as former Institute of the History of the USSR), the Center for the Research of North-Eastern Asia at the Academy of Social Sciences in Jilin province, the Institute of Nationalities, the Institute of History, and the Institute of Archeology, Religion, and the Research of Middle Asia, a part of the Academy of Social Sciences of the Xinjiang-Uigur autonomous region.

Studies in the field have also been pursued in the departments or specialized research institutes of the universities, pedagogical institutes (usually in the departments of history) and institutes of foreign languages in such provinces as Inner Mongolia, Liaoning, Xinjiang, Heilongjiang, Jilin, Shaanxi, Sichuan and in major cities such as Beijing, Tianjin, Xian, Harbin, Shanghai, etc. Research on Sino-Russian relations is coordinated by the Provincial Associations of Sino-Russian Relations which were created in most of the Chinese provinces, the Northeast Association of Sino-Russian Relations and the Association of Chinese Historians.

Despite the potential for appropriate direction and intensive analysis these centers and coordinating bodies offer, it is important to stress that they all operate under specific circumstances where ideological concerns are given priority. Any authoritarian regime raises serious questions about the problem of bias in the social sciences and casts doubt on the veracity of historical analysis. Historiography in China has always been highly ideological and ethnocentric; dissident ideas that did not correspond to "official" facts have been systematically eliminated. For thousands of years, the writing of history in China has been a process of interpreting events to serve specific political purposes. Each new emperor has commissioned scholars to recast the previous reign according to his interests. The current regime has followed in this tradition, making the possibility of "balanced" research still problematic.

The questions raised concerning Sino-Russian relations have been just as seriously considered in the former Soviet Union and to a lesser extent because of financial difficulties, in today's Russia.

Though there were and still are many publications on this theme in the former Soviet Union, it is important to stress that writing on Sino-Russian history in Russia has never been a part of the state historiography as it was and still is in China. In Russia, these writings were more the efforts of separate individuals, sometimes strongly influenced by government interests or contrary to mainstream historical ideas, than the efforts

---

[22] The second largest national department is located here.

of the state to interpret the history of its relationship with its neighbors. The specialized academic center "Russia - China" is functioning at the Institute of Far Eastern Studies (Russian Academy of Sciences), while some researchers specializing in the history of Sino-Russian relations and international relations in Central Asia are working also at the Institute of Oriental Studies, Institute of History (Russian Academy of Sciences), all based in Moscow. Some researchers are still working in other cities of Russia (St. Petersburg, Khabarovsk, Vladivostok) and the new Central Asian states (Almaty, Bishkek, Tashkent). The problems connected with Sino-Russian relations are being discussed in Russia by different panels of conferences of the Russian Association of Chinese Studies, and at annual conferences: "State and Society in China," "China and the World" and "The Skachkov Conferences" (*Skachkovskii Chteniya*). Russian scholars are publishing a unique documentary series of academic books "Sino-Russian Relations," which is introducing into scholarly analysis a large amount of previously unpublished Russian archival materials as well as documents relating to Sino-Russian relations and translated from Chinese, Manchu and Western languages.[23] The collapse of the Soviet Union has made it possible for Russian scholars to perpetuate different concepts. But these new Russian approaches are very fragile because the whole Russian state is in a process of searching for a national identity. They are very vulnerable to the current political struggles in Russia and the lack of financial support for social sciences from non-government resources. The last reason explains why many interesting conceptual innovations in Russia have never been published.

---

[23] *Russko-Kitaiskiye Otnosheniya v XVII V. Materialy i Dokumenty* (Russian-Chinese Relations in the 17th Century. Materials and Documents). Vol. 1. (1608-1683). Moscow, 1969; Vol. 2 (1685-1691). Moscow. 1972; *Russko-Kitaiskiye Otnoshenoya v XVIII V.Materialy i Dokumenty.* (Russian-Chinese Relations in the 18th Century. Materials and Documents). Vol. 1. (1700-1725). Moscow, 1978 etc.

THE PROBLEM OF SOURCES

The primary sources in the field of Sino-Russian relations can be grouped into three areas according to their linguistic origin:

1. **Chinese sources.**
2. **Russian sources.**
3. **Sources in Western European languages** (and other languages such as **Tibetan, Turkish,** etc.).

Each of these three main groups can be further divided into four subcategories:

1. **Archival documents and materials.**
2. **Official chronicles.**
3. **Compilations of documents** (official and unofficial).
4. **Authored works.** These include memoirs, biographies, autobiographies, and personal documents.

I will concentrate here mostly on Chinese primary sources because scholars regard these as the most reliable published primary sources and because the metatheoretical (methodological) problems arising around this whole group of materials should be analyzed.

Primary sources in Western European languages are important, although they must be treated as supplementary, insofar as they are useful only indirectly for substantiating other primary materials. Their direct use is limited to cases when Western powers were involved in Sino-Russian relations. Such an example would be the so-called "Ili Crisis" (1871-1881) where Great Britain played a central role.[24] Western primary sources include government archives (especially those of foreign offices), published collections of documents and materials,[25] and personal memoirs and private letters.[26] Sources in other languages (Tibetan, Turkish, etc.) are also very valuable, primarily because they are an alternative source of information and allow scholars to compare the way facts were arranged in Chinese historiography.[27]

Russian archival materials (especially those located in the Archives of the Russian Empire's Foreign Policy) are tremendously important, providing one of most objective pictures of China's history at the time. These materials have been catalogued in the archives on a day by day, month by month, and year by year basis. All are cataloged in their original form.[28] Russian diplomatic representatives in China prepared detailed reports and therefore provided a relatively accurate picture of international relations in the region though obviously from the standpoint of Russian interests.[29] In addition, Russian archives have a very substantial collection of Chinese documents and diplomatic papers (some in their original form, but mostly as copies) that can sufficiently substantiate Russian documents. Interestingly, Chinese authorities still kept tight their own government archives' collections on Sino-Russian relations to foreign researchers.[30] Russian archives were opened[31] several years ago to the public and an extensive amount of this material is being published.[32]

---

[24] See, for example, I. Hsu. *The Ili Crisis. A Study of Sino-Russian Diplomacy. 1871-1881.* Oxford. 1966 and A. Voskressenski. *The Sino-Russian St.Petersburg Treaty of 1881 - Diplomatic History.* Nova Science Publishers, Inc., NY (forthcoming).

[25] *Die Grosse Politik Der Europaishen Kabinette. 1871-1914.* Berlin. 1922-1924; S.Y.Couvrier. *Choix Des Documents. Lettres, Officielles Proclamations, Edits, Memorieux ets.* Ho Kien-Fau. 1901; Ed. Hertslet (ed.) *Treaties etc. between Great Britain and China; and Between China and Foreign Powers...* London. 1896; W. McMurray. *Treaties and Agreements with and Concerning China. 1894-1914.* New York. 1921; *Treaties,Conventions etc. Between China and Foreign Powers.* Shanghai. 1917. etc.

[26] For example, J.K. Fairbank, K.F. Bruner, E.M. Matheson. *The I.G. in Peking. Letters of Robert Hart.* Cambridge. 1975.

[27] Unfortunately not many scholars use these sources because it implies aknowledge of at least two 'Oriental' languages.

[28] For a description of Russian archival materials on Sino-Russian relations see: *Pussko-Kitayskie Otnosheniya v 17 Veke* (Sino-Russian Relations in the 17th Century). Vol. I. 1608-1683. Moscow. 1969; *Russko-Kitayskie Otnosheniya v 18 Veke.* (Sino-Russian Relations in the 18th Century). Vol. 2. 1685-1691. Moscow. 1972; *Russko-Kitayskie otnosheniya v 18 Veke.* (Sino-Russian Relations in the 18th Century). Vol. I. 1700-1725. Moscow. 1978.

[29] The standpoint of state interests renders relatively accurate reports since misrepresentation of foreign relations make the implementation of rational decisions very difficult.

[30] For example, though there were very interesting materials on Sino-Russian relations in the Russian language in Chinese archives seen by some Russians researchers in the 1950's during the close friendship between Soviet Union and China, these collections are very difficult to penetrate until today as far as I know.

Other Russian materials include various collections of treaties, agreements, and memoirs of people who participated in the events.[33] Usually these materials are not based on the state interpretation of the events and therefore provide a relatively balanced illustration of the international relations in the region.

The most significant and reliable archival materials, however, have one "weak" point -- in order to gain access, a scholar must go to the country where the archives are located. As of yet, there is no procedure for copying these materials, and any published collection of archival documents raises the question of the method for selection and so also of possible bias.

In the following section, I have devised a **systematization** of Chinese primary sources of the Qing period (the sources of this period survey 90% of the period of Sino-Russian relations). The system is intended as a preliminary phase before formal classification.[34] Classification is a sophisticated and complicated process and consists at least of four stages:

1. definition of the domain of classification;
2. grouping of the elements into sets;
3. labeling of the groups;
4. arrangement of the categories in the appropriate order (in hierarchical order, for example).[35]

Systematization, on the other hand, is a much simpler process consisting of grouping the elements into sets and labeling these groups. Appropriate systematization is necessary, because from the conceptual point of view it reflects the researcher's approach to the "raw material," i.e., to the basic primary sources.

Many Russian scholars use a simple classification of Chinese sources of the Qing period that consists of three categories: imperial chronicles (*shilu*), official or standard histories (*zhengshi*) and unofficial (dissident)

---

[31] The decision to completely open the Russian archives is very important. Every publication raises the question of bias which will remain until all the documents are available for criticism by other specialists.

[32] See, for example, the above-mentioned series of academic books on Sino-Russian relations published in Russia.

[33] These books are usually reviewed in historiographical sections of Russian books or Ph.D dissertations on the theme.

[34] R. Sokal. "Classification: Purposes, Principles, Progress, Prospects". *Science 185*. 1974. P. 115-23.

[35] P. Starr. "The Sociology of Statistics" (P.44) in W. Alonzo and P. Starr. *The Politics of Numbers*. New York. 1987.

histories (*yeshi*).³⁶ Others use a more detailed classification system such as W. Franke's classification of Ming sources based on the metatheoretical approach, which, with corrections, can also be used for the Qing period. His classification consists of nine main categories (each of which is divided into several subcategories):

1. Government publications of historical sources;
2. Semi-official works on individual government agencies and institutions;
3. Semi-private and private historiography in the composite and analytic styles;
4. Biographical writing;
5. Various notes dealing with historical subjects;
6. Writing on state affairs;
7. Works on foreign affairs and on military organizations;
8. Encyclopedias and works on geography, economics, and technology;
9. Works on local history.³⁷

Many Chinese scholars employ more detailed classifications, reflecting their better familiarization with Chinese sources.³⁸

Good systematization or classification should avoid these two extremes; a classification consisting of only three categories is only useful as a general approach to the sources while a classification which is too detailed lacks an interpretive base. A distinction should be made in a systematization between more important primary sources and less important ones.³⁹ This distinction ensures that a researcher does not miss grouping important sources together in the same category, highlighting their priority. It also allows a researcher to cross-reference his/her main materials, and on the base of such correlation, to judge the accuracy of each particular source.

---

³⁶ B.G. Doronin. "Chinese State Historiography of the 17th Century". *17 Nauchnaya Konferentsiya "Obschestvo i Gosudarstvo v Kitaye"*. Hereafter referred to only in English with consequent number: 17th Academic Conference "State and Society in China". Moscow. 1981.

³⁷ W. Franke. "Historical Writing during the Ming Period". *The Cambridge History of China*. Vol. 7. Part I. Cambridge University Press. 1988.

³⁸ Chen Gaohua, Chen Zhizhao. *Zhongguo Gudaishi Shiliaoxue*. (Researches on the Sources in Ancient China). Beijing. 1983; Chen Gonglu (ed.) *Zhongguo Jindaishi Ziliao Gaishu*.(General Description of Chinese Materials on Modern History). Beijing. 1982.

³⁹ Such systematization, which is as relatively subjective as all others seems to be more 'objective' if is created on the base of the dichotomy of "subjectiveness-objectiveness", where the most 'objective' group of materials are Archives.

I have systematized Chinese primary sources of the Qing period that can be used for the analysis of the Sino-Russian relations, in the following manner[40]:

1. *Archival Documents and Materials.*
2. *Official Chronicles (Shilu).*
3. *Various Compilations of Documents.* This category consists of the following subcategories: **compilation of laws** (*huidian, huidian shili*) and **rules** of the various departments and directorates, like *Libu Zeli* (The Rules Set by the Department of Ceremonial) or *Lifanyuan Zeli* (The Rules Established by the Department [of the Lands] of Vassals); **compilation of documents** such as *fangüe* (strategic plans) and *jiüe* (strategic records), which had been established after every major military campaign to add glory and legitimacy to the ruling emperor; **chronicles of local areas, historic-geographical descriptions of particular territories** or **the works on geography and territorial administration** (*fangzhi, difangzhi, tujing*); and **the reports, memorials,** and memoranda to the Emperor of famous officials (*zougao, zouyi*).
4. *Authored works.* This category consists of authored historical works (**histories**), and can be divided into **official** or standard histories or (accounts) (*zhengshi*) and **unofficial** (dissident) histories (*yeshi*); various **authorsed works**: including **genealogies** (*nianpu, jiapu*), collections of **literary works** (*wenji*) including political essays in which researcher always can find elements of theoretical thinking, and **unofficial** (dissident) **records** (*yeji*), usually organized around a particular theme. **Memoirs** and **diaries** (*riji, biji, huilu*) also constitute a subcategory of authors' works.

Chinese scholars currently use practically all of the above-mentioned categories, relying in particular on the most important of these, the *Chronicles (Qing Shilu).*[41] The importance of *Shilu* derives from the fact that there are no modern systematic publications of Chinese archival materials. Publications of archival materials are organized on an ad-hoc basis and are based on differing classifications and rules. This lack of standardization means that all non-Chronicle collections of documents can at best substantiate, but never substitute, the materials contained in *Shilu*. The

---

[40] I tried to make the systematization more universal in order to make possible the correlation between sources in different languages.

[41] The exact translation is: "Records of Deeds of the Qing Dynasty" but can also be loosely translated as "Veritable Records".

new publication of *Chronicles* is located in all serious research libraries that have an Asian collection of books.

Since early times, the keeping of chronicles was considered an important function of Chinese government. The special Bureau or Committee of Historiography (*Goushiguan*), established during the first half of the seventh century, compiled the records on which the national official history (*guoshi*) and standard histories (*zhengshi*) were based. This Bureau continued to function in later periods. Official historiographers collected documents, materials and made compilations of historical records. In line with ancient tradition, one of the most important functions of these "history" officials was to keep records of imperial life, i.e., imperial audiences, edicts, memorials and memoranda, etc. Given that the compilation of *Shilu* was primarily of a political nature and not, "simply" academic, modern researchers must take into account the probability of political bias and try to identify the context and implications of these biases.

The text of *Qing Shilu* was published by Japanese scholars between 1933 and 1937 (photostatic reprint of the original text).[42] Between 1965 and 1975, Taiwanese scholars made a second reprint of the *Qing Chronicles*. Scholars in the People's Republic of China have republished various parts of the *Shilu* including sections on economics. The entire *Qing Shilu* was expertly published in the People's Republic of China between 1985 and 1987.[43]

The "classic" Japanese publication was based on the text that has been kept in Shenyang, but China's publishers also used the Beijing variant in their publication. This new publication is actually based on the "Beijing text" (3,417 Chinese volumes or *juan*); the second part is also "Beijing text," although it has also been taken from another place - the Gugong Imperial Palace (349 volumes). The third part comes from the library of Beijing University. The initial 4,333 volumes have been reorganized into 60 books.[44]

---

[42] *Dai Qing Lichao Shilu*. Vol. 1-94. Tokyo.1937.

[43] About the publication see: Chen Gaohua, Chen Zhizhao. *Zhongguo Gudaishi Shiliaoxue*.

[44] For a complete description of *Qing Shilu* as a source see: W.Fuks. "Zur Druckausgabe Der Shih-Lu Der Manju-Dinastie". *Monumenta Serica*. 1983. #9; K. Biggerstaff. "Some Notes on the Tong-Hua Lu and the Shih-Lu". *Harvard Journal of Asiatic Studies*. Vol. 4. #2; G. Melikhov. "Dai Qing Lichao Shilu" as a Historical Source. *Strany Dalnego Vostoka i Yugo-Vostochnoi Azii*. (The Countries of the Far East and of the South-East Asia). Moscow. 1969; see also my article "Dai Qing Lichao Shilu" as a Source on the History of International Relations in Central Asia". *17th Academic Conference "State and Society in China"*. Moscow. 1986, introduction to my above-mentioned forthcoming book on St. Petersburg Treaty and my co-authored preface to the book *Mezhdunarodnie Otnosheniya v Tsentralnoi Azii*. (The International Relations in Central Asia). Vol. 1. Moscow. 1989.

It is known that five copies of the *Shilu* were originally written in the Chinese, the Mongolian and the Manchu languages. These copies were kept in four different sites within two separate cities: Beijing and Shenyang. All these variants are now collected in The First Historical Archive in Beijing and the Liaoning Archive.

Some scholars argue that variants in different languages are totally identical.[45] I think, however, this is unlikely. For example, it is known that the Chinese text of *Manchou Shilu* (one of the variants of *Taizu Shilu*) differs from the Manchu text in the historical details (especially descriptions), transcription of names, titles, etc.[46] It is also known that three variants of *Taizu Gaohuangdi (Nuerhaqi) Shilu* exist and all three were published in Taiwan and on mainland China.[47] The significance of the differences in these three texts of *Shilu* is still unresolved. At the same time given the so-called "half-closed" character of the source, the fact that very few changes can be made once an official version has been written, and the huge number of volumes, it seems reasonable to assume that these changes were the result of rather small corrections in the official chronicles.

The relative accuracy of *Shilu* is bolstered by the fact that the texts were never intended for publication, although at the same time, they were never completely secret. *Shilu* was written for an inner circle of Chinese elites, including the emperor himself, members of his family, and top state officials. *Shilu* was a kind of encyclopedia on Chinese domestic and international policy and served as a basis of policy formation. The fact that *Shilu* was written for a political elite makes it more reliable as a source for modern analysts. Having said this, however, it must be remembered that *Shilu* represents the official version of all events and therefore that it is concerned much more with the emperor's edicts than with the political or social history of China. Furthermore, since an official editorial body chose the documents and materials to be included in *Shilu*, the method of choice reflects the very large problem of bias. Written imperial edicts and various memoranda were also obviously abridged, altering the picture of historical events. Simultaneously, the extremely diverse character of the materials found in *Shilu* makes this source basic for all researchers. W.Franke, an international expert on Chinese historiography of the Ming period, writes of *Ming Shilu*.[48]:

---

[45] For example, Russian historian G. Melikhov. (See his above-mentioned article).

[46] The evidence for this comes from the official seals on the text.

[47] Chen Gaohua, Chen Zhizhao. *Zhongguo Gudaishi Shiliaoxue*. P.438-439.

[48] All of the principles for compiling official records were the same for the Ming as for the Qing dynasties.

"In a strictly chronological order of year, month, and day, the veritable records reported all the actions undertaken by the emperor or in the name of the emperor, as well as important political events. These records naturally tend to contain information that would be useful to the imperial government. The recorded facts appear mostly in the form of excerpts from memorials, for the events were reported in this way to the throne by officials in charge, and from relevant imperial orders. Moreover, appointments, transfers, or suspensions of higher officials are usually noted, as are startling natural phenomena.

Events, however, are not necessarily recorded under the date on which they actually occurred, but under the day on which they were reported and discussed in imperial audiences. If things happened at a distant place, a considerable amount of time might elapse between the date on which the event occurred and the date on which it was brought up at court. Under the date on which the death of high official was reported, a short biography was usually appended. At the end of each year, statistical data on the population, on tax revenues, on foreign "tribute" embassies, and so on, were given.

It is evident from the organization of the compilation of the veritable records in Ming times that it was an important political task. Some of the supervisors and compilers were severely reproached by later writers for showing partiality according to their personal sympathies and aversions. Since the veritable records are for the most part made up from the texts of official documents and from dry reports about government actions, the chances for the author to express his personal opinion rested mainly in the selection of some documents and in the suppression of others. In this way, facts and events could be greatly misrepresented... If the documents themselves (memorials, for example) contained erroneous statements, it was not the duty of the compilers to correct these..."[49]

Shilu, of course, is not the only Chinese source that can be used for research in the field of the history of Sino-Russian border relations. Scholars can also use different compilations of documents similar to but smaller than *Shilu*[50] including collections dealing with the foreign policy of the Qing dynasty such as *Chouban Yiwu Shimo* (Complete Plans for Ruling the Barbarians) and *Qingji Waijiao Shiliao* (Materials on the Foreign Relations of the Qing Period). There are also collections concerned specially with

---

[49] W. Franke. "Historical Writing during the Ming Period". *The Cambridge History of China*. P.747-748.

[50] *Donghualu* (Records from the Donghua Pavilion). Beijing. 1984. (Reprint of the original edition); *Guangxuchao Donghualu* (Records from the Donghua Pavilion of the Guanxu Reign). Beijing. 1984. (Reprint of the original edition).

Sino-Russian relations,[51] which like *Chouban Yiwu Shimo* and *Qingji Waijiao Shiliao* are similar in some ways to *Shilu*, but organized around a particular theme[52] rather than represent general history. *Qingji Waijiao Shiliao* was first published in the 1930s, i.e., many years after the fall of the Qing dynasty. Although the timing of publication suggests more objectivity than *Shilu*, the principles of compilation were practically the same as for the *Veritable Records*.

Qingji Waijiao Shiliao contains various reports of state officials to the emperor or to the Main Directorate of Foreign Affairs (*Zongliyamen*) in connection to different political or social events, for example, the arrival of distinguished foreign visitors, etc. These documents can be substantiated by various compilations of reports prepared by leading Chinese officials including Li Hongzhang, Zuo Zongtang, and Zeng Jize who all wrote on foreign policy issues.[53]

In addition to *Shilu*, there are two other important secondary sources, *Qingshi Gao* (The Draft History of the Qing Dynasty),[54] and *Qingshi* (The Qing History). These histories do not provide new information but are useful for comparison with *Qing Shilu*.[55]

Memoirs, diaries and other unofficial works are especially useful for understanding how official Chinese history has been created. Research based on these types of sources is still very new, however, therefore many problems raised by subjective sources have yet to be addressed.

Practically all these sources were either analyzed or mentioned in the introductions to the primary books on Chinese history, international relations (including history of the Sino-Russian relations) and historiography. Many quotations appear in the main body of these texts. Nevertheless, the problem of the correlation between bias and state interests in traditional sources has practically never been seriously analyzed by Chinese researchers.

Central to the problem of bias is the general question about the issues that have been considered major in the historiography of the Qing period. This is a particularly important question for researchers concerned with Qing China's relations with other states as well as with Russia. Keeping in

---

[51] He Qutao. *Shuofang Beisheng*. (The Description of the Northern Regions). Wood engraved text. No publication place and date available.

[52] *Chouban Yiwu Shimo*. No publication place available. 1857-1881; *Qingji Waijiao Shiliao*. Beijing. 1930.

[53] *Li Wenzhong Quanji*. (Complete Works by Li Hongzhang). Shanghai. 1925; *Zuo Wenxianggong Quanji*. (Complete Works by Zuo Zongtang). (?). 1890; *Zeng Huimingong Yiji*. (Works by Zeng Zize). Taipei. 1968.

[54] Especially important are the chapters of this "collective history" which are dedicated to the relationship between China, Russia and the Western powers.

[55] *Qingshigao*. Beijing. 1927; *Qingshi*. Taipei. 1927.

mind how Qing scholars understood the historical process, balanced research is essential. As a way of interpreting the goals of the chronicles and other sources, researchers should compare Chinese official sources with unofficial (dissident) sources, many of which have been substantiated with Russian archival materials. This type of comparison and juxtaposition can reveal the hidden motives and underlying reasons behind Chinese sources. Unfortunately the overwhelming majority of Chinese unofficial histories for the Qing period were destroyed by the dynasty's so-called "literary inquisition." This is not facilitating the analysis.

In analyzing historical fact or events, researchers proceed *a priori* from the assumption that no one source alone can ever be sufficient for the reliable reconstruction of the moving forces in history. Interestingly, this assumption was stressed by several Chinese historians writing during Qing period. Many unorthodox scholars, especially during the early Qing regime, were very skeptical about the official (standard) history (*zhengshi*). Unfortunately, there are virtually no statements by Qing historians still in existence concerning the historiography of their own dynasty, primarily because of the "literary inquisition." Well-known historians, like Wang Shizhen, Shen Dafu, Zhang Dai etc., by using various euphemisms and Aesopian language however, were long ago able to criticize the official approach to the history of the previous Ming dynasty, but not of the ruling Qing dynasty.

Any researcher who uses Chinese sources must recognize that in China historical facts were recorded only when they had an appropriate ideological accent, - i.e., when the fact corresponded to an appropriate political position. Facts that otherwise had no political value were rejected. In China, histories are considered "reliable" when historians had rejected "private" or subjective views and instead, offered a "standard", i.e., officially correct interpretation.

Unfortunately, most Chinese scholars, even today, do not use metatheoretical or methodological approaches[56] in their work, and instead, base their research on the official Chinese version of events. In this way they perpetuate the same approach to history practiced in China since ancient times. All other sources (Russian as well as Western) are used to "prove" this standard version, i.e., Chinese scholars take from these sources only the facts that correspond to their conceptions, rejecting as non-reliable or ignoring all other material. This approach renders Chi-

---

[56] Except common phrases implying the importance of the implementation of the Chinese interpretation of Marxism for Social Sciences. The implications of the Marxist vision are analyzed in - Arif Dirlik. Revolution and History. The origins of Marxist Historiography in China, 1919-1937. U. of California Press, 1978.

nese historiography highly ideological. In the next sections I will try to show how this ideological approach influences and distorts scholarly research.

Simultaneously, the same is correct for Russian researchers writing on the history of Sino-Russian relations. Being aware of the metatheoretical weakness of the Chinese sources and usually successfully reconstructing historical fact "trimmed" in official Chinese chronicles, they failed to interpret it correctly, ceding to the temptation of explaining all events from the standpoint of Russian state interests. Most of them for decades considered the Russian and the Soviet empires' policy as wholly representing Russian national interests. It was only after the collapse of the Soviet Union that researchers in Russia began to seriously investigate the problems of perceived Russian national interests and the interests of other nations compared with the state interests of the Russian empire as a whole.

CHINESE APPROACHES

A. CHINESE CONCEPTIONS OF SINO-RUSSIAN RELATIONS AND BORDER PROBLEMS (1980-1990)

1. DOMINANT PARADIGM

Before analyzing Chinese attitudes and assumptions concerning Sino-Russian relations and border problems, it is important to explore the metatheoretical questions encountered in this area, that is the mainstream Chinese concept of a "united multinational China," which gained additional prominence in the 1970s and was further elaborated upon in the 1980s. There are two variations of this paradigm.[57] The first, which is also the most academically rigorous, argues that the formation of modern China is the result of a long, complicated and contradictory process of historical development. The second - and more popular variation - differs markedly from the first. Rather than placing the formation of the Chinese state into a historical context, it argues that China has been a "united and multinational" state from the very beginning of Chinese civilization. In this variation scholars project modern Chinese history back into the past — explaining the development of the ancient Chinese with modern ideological considerations. This variation rejects the idea that state frontiers evolve during the course of history. It assumes that all of the nations involved in tributary relations with the Han (Chinese) nationality were integral parts of a "unified and multinational" Chinese empire.

There is an obvious similarity between the Chinese concept of a "united multinational China" and the Soviet idea of "the Soviet people as a

---

[57] Soviet reaction to this concept is developed in: L.S. Perelomov, S.N. Goncharov, E.V. Nikogosov. "The Great Han Character of 'Eternal Multinational China' Paradigm". *Problemy Dalnego Vostoka* . #3. 1981.

new historical union of different nationalities." The emergence of these kinds of concepts can be traced to the functional necessity of a unifying ideology in an authoritarian state. Unifying ideologies are needed to justify empires composed of disparate nationalities. Therefore, although the views presented by Soviet and Chinese historiography to Sino-Russian relations and border problems are diametrically opposed in a sense that both sides simply blamed each other for the aggressive policy toward their neighbor, these approaches are nevertheless typologically very similar. This fact has made the search for a neutral and more balanced interpretation of the mutual history of these two states very difficult, if possible at all. Historical analysis in both countries has been based on the assumption that the assimilation of small, local nationalities was progressive in history and benevolent to them; Imperialists' projects have been ignored and the significance of China and Russia in world history has been superficially strengthened, insofar as historical events have been redefined and subordinated to the historical endeavor of the two states.

The ideological confrontation that had occurred between the USSR and China within the last decade has greatly influenced the emergence of these deformed histories. Developments in Europe and Asia, including the breakdown of totalitarian states and the increasing demands for democratization, have exposed these simple ideological characterizations to intense criticism. It is unlikely that the kinds of assumptions made within such historical concepts will survive the unprecedented changes occurring in Europe and -- to a lesser degree -- in Asia. In Russia all ideological approaches to the history are rejected by the academic community though the interpretation of the history by political leaders is still highly ideological. In China also the dominant historiographical paradigm is beginning slowly to break down in the academic community though this process is still indecisive.

During the 1980s a series of authors was published in China which further elaborated on the argument of a "united multinational China," or a "united Chinese nation." This idea has become the methodological base for all Chinese research on medieval China and the Qing period.[58] Although the central axiom of this concept that China is the product of all nationalities currently living within the modern state's territorial boundaries is

---

[58] See, for example, "Creation of the United Multinational State in the Song Era". *Jiefangjun Huabao*. #10. 1984; Lü, Changyi. "Fostering Patriotism in Teaching Chinese Modern History". *Jiaoyu yu Yanjiu*. #2. 1984; Li Jipin. "Unification of China during the Beginning of the Qing Dynasty under the Reign of the Emperor Shunzhi (1638-1661). *Shixue Yuekan*. #2. 1984; "Patriotism of Different Nationalities in their Struggle for Unification of the State in Chinese History". *Beifang Luncun*. #5. 1984; Cai Jingfu. "Relationship between Different Nationalities in Chinese History". *Beifang Luncun*. #6. 1984.

very controversial and can be easily criticized, this conception is, nonetheless, crucially important for building a national identity.[59] While aware of this, Chinese scholars have recently started to criticize the historical accuracy of this conception. Although this criticism is still very new, it is an important indicator of possible changes in the future, since it suggests undercurrent revisionism.

Analyses based on this dominant paradigm have provided the scholarly basis for research into questions relating to border problems and other issues. These general analyses include: "Distinctions between the National Question in Different Historical Periods are Needed,[60]" an article written by an anonymous Chinese author, in which "national clashes and national contacts" from the Qin (221-207 B.C.) and Han (206 B.C.-220) dynasties up to the Qing dynasty are seen as "the building and strengthening of the national state.[61]" Similar ideas are developed by Su Shuangbi in his article "Studies on the History of National Relations," and by Guo Dehong and Li Minsan in their article "The Unification of the Country is an Inevitable Trend of the Historical Development of the Chinese Nation,[62]" where it is argued that contemporary China is the historical successor to the medieval Chinese empire. Pen Inmin and Xu Jieshun, authors of "Concerning the Formation of United Multinational China,[63]" try to prove that the "intimate economic and cultural contacts between different nationalities in the northern regions of China were the basis of the formation of a united multinational state.[64]" Other examples include Tong Zhuchen's article "The Historical Contribution of the Nationalities of the Border Areas of China,[65]" Li Bangzheng's article "About the National Hero, National Honor and Patriotism in Chinese History"[66] etc. A common theme in these articles is the emphasis on the "historical contribution" of various nationalities "to the defence of the motherland's unity.[67]" It should be stressed

---

[59] In Russian historiography this conclusion was formulated first by B.G. Doronin in his article "Modern Stage of Studies of Qing History in the People's Republic of China". *Novoe v Izuchenii Kitaya* (New Concepts in Chinese Studies). Moscow. 1988.

[60] *Yunnan Minzu Xueyuan Xuebao.* #1. 1983.

[61] *Zhongguo Lishi Nianjian* (Chinese Historical Sciences. A Year Book). Beijing. 1984. P.175.

[62] *Yunnan Minzu Xueyuan Xuebao.* #1. 1983; *Hongqi.* #3. 1984.

[63] *Beifang Lunqun.* #1. 1983.

[64] *Zhongguo Lishi Nianjian.* P.175.

[65] *Heilongjiang Wenwu Cunkan.* #1. 1983.

[66] *Qushi Xuekan.* #5. 1983.

[67] Guo Yunhua. "Common Struggle of all Nationalities of Xinjiang during the Han Epoch for the Defence of the Motherland". *Zhongyang Minzuxueyuan Xuebao.* #4. 1983; Lü Guitian. "Historical Role of Evenks in the

this way that most of these nationalities are divided and are living on both sides of the former Sino-Soviet border. The attempts to "include" them into the "history of the Chinese nation" are still considered in Central Asia and Russia as attempts to undermine current borders between Russia, China and the new Central Asian states.

Virtually all of the studies on China's modern history and on problems concerning international relations include special sections describing the history of Sino-Russian contacts. These sections are written from the point of view which recognizes a "united Chinese nation" and therefore seriously overestimates the integrity of China's territorial boundaries, implying that these boundaries have been historically static.

It is important to stress that most scholars attempting to analyze the history of Sino-Russian relations eventually come to the conclusion that the characterization of these relations is a central question, since the approach to this problem is indicative of the entire process by which the history of Sino-Russian relations should be interpreted. The question of characterization is followed precisely by the question of the perceived equality or inequality of the Sino-Russian treaties. These questions are so important because unlike the Sino-Western treaties of the past, the Sino-Russian treaties established the Sino-Russian border that later become the Sino-Soviet border, which is now the border between Russia, China and the new Central Asian states. The border articles of the 19th century treaties are valid till now. Chinese scholars operating within the dominant paradigm proceed from the assumption that all Sino-Russian treaties, except the early ones that were signed during clear Chinese dominance in the region (The Treaties of Nerchinsk and Burinsk), were biased against China, - i.e., were imposed by an aggressive Russian government. In the Soviet Union and Russia this concept is considered as an attempt to find a historical legacy to undermine the current borders and ask for compensation. Russia is represented in these analyses as the singular constant within the historical process without taking into consideration any external forces and domestic political struggles that shaped Russian attitudes toward the neighbors. Russian foreign policy is presented in a primitive, oversimplified manner with a superficial accent on Russian violence. In contrast, the policy of the Manchu emperors is idealized as a counterbalance against the "aggressive course" of the Russian state.

Although simplistic and superficial, this concept of unequal relations is based, to a very large degree, on real "experience" (i.e., some historical

---

Preservation of the Motherland and Defence of its Borders during the Ming Era. *Xuexi yu Tansuo*. #3. 1984; Li Guihai. "Patriotic Struggle of Different Nationalities in Chinese History". *Beifang Luncun*. #5. 1984.

facts). In certain key historical periods China has indeed been the much weaker state vis à vis Russia. It does not follow from this, however, that paradigms based on elements of truth are immune to criticism. It must be remembered that the focus of social sciences is on the belief that "truth" (in a philosophical sense) is arrived at in the interplay of different, even contradictory ideas.

2. ATTITUDES TOWARD IMPERIAL RUSSIA

Chinese scholarship portrays Imperial Russia as an aggressive, violent and expansionist state. For example, in the book *Short History of Foreign Countries*[68] a special chapter is devoted to the description of the "external expansion of the Russian tsars.[69]" The authors of this book stress that after the reign of Tsar Ivan IV, Russia began to pursue "the foreign policy of expansion," and that this new policy reflected the desire of its leaders to transform Russia from an "internal country to a modernized force." "The expansionist character" of Russia's Far Eastern policy is explained as the result of defeats Russia suffered in the West and South. These defeats convinced Russia's leaders of the need to reassert their country's military and foreign policy efforts.

Chinese scholars argue that from the middle of the 17th century, Russia began to intrude into the Heilongjiang region of China,[70] attempting to find a gateway to the Pacific Ocean. Military detachments of Tsarist Russia are accused of "violently eliminating" the population of these Chinese border territories and "of occupying the large territories to the north of the Heilongjiang (Amur) River and to the east of the Ussuri River." At the same time Russia's military is condemned, Chinese detachments are applauded for "rebuffing Russian aggression." The victorious Qing army is also praised for forcing Russia to accept the Treaty of Nerchinsk spelling out new border regulations favorable to the Chinese empire.[71]

The same argument appears in the official *World History*[72] textbook used in Chinese schools. In the textbook version, 17th century Russia is portrayed as the "huge, dangerous, northern neighbor" of China, and the 19th century predecessor is accused of being the "main agent of the divi-

---

[68] Li Zuxun. Lü Mingyuan. *Waiguo Lishi Changyi*. (History of Foreign Countries). Beijing. 1982.

[69] Ibid. P. 193-6.

[70] Heilongjiang means the whole basin of the Heilongjiang (Amur) river.

[71] *Ibid.* P. 196.

[72] *Shijie Lishi* . Beijing. 1986.

sion of China." Russia is characterized as having pursued a foreign policy based entirely on international aggression for more than three hundred years. According to standard Chinese histories, the target of Russian tsarist foreign policy was always "the achievement of world hegemony.[73]" Chinese historians argue that "Russia's expansion into the Orient, which began in the 17th century, accelerated the process of the primary accumulation of Russian capital and therefore, the development of Russia's capitalist economy.[74]" According to the authors, beginning in the 18th century, "Russian capital accumulation was based on the sweat and blood" of the people of Siberia, Central Asia and China.[75]

3. NATIONAL HISTORIES

During the last ten years, Chinese scholars have become very interested in the history of the small ethnic groups, which were, and in many cases, are still living along both sides of China's current border with Russia and the new Central Asian states. Much of this recent scholarship has attempted to show that these small nationalities have always been "under the rule" or "within the sphere of influence" of the Chinese empire, and that in those cases where these peoples are now living in other states, that their territories were taken by force. Studies of these kinds include: *The Short History of Orochens, The Short History of Tajiks, The History of the Economic Development of Inner Mongolia, The History of Uigur, The History of Dzungars*[76] etc.

Research into the social organization of these small nationalities was transformed into a kind of "half-independent" scholarly field in the late 1980s[77] and attempts to show that the structural character of these people's social institutions provides proof that they were at one time a part

---

[73] *Ibid.* P. 55. The same conception is elaborated in the book *Diguozhuyi Qin Hua Zuixinlu*. (Dossier of Crimes of the Imperialist Aggression in China). Jinan. 1986.

[74] Bo Sunming. Feng Xisheng. "Analysis of the Interrelationship between the Aggression of Russia in the 'Oriental' Direction and the Initial Capitalist Accumulation". *Beijing Shifan Daxue.* #2. 1985. A review of this article was published in *Zhongguo Lishi.* #3. 1986.

[75] Ibid. P. 145.

[76] *Olunchun Jianshi* (Short History of the Orochens). Khukh-Khoto. 1983; *Tajikezu Jianshi* (History of the Tajiks). Urumchi. 1983; *Nei Menggu Jingji Fazhanshi* (History of the Economic Development of Inner Mongolia). Khukh-Khoto. 1983; *Weiwuerzu Shi* (History of the Uigurs). Beijing. 1985; *Zhonggeer Shilue.* (History of the Dzungars). Beijing. 1985.

[77] *Zhongguo Lishi Nianjian.* 1984. P. 178-80.

either of the Chinese civilization or at least within the sphere of Chinese "cultural influence."[78]

Other works dealing with the question of nationality are comprised of this same type of bias. In his article "Historical Heritage and Patriotism," published in *Guangming Ribao* in 1983, Lin Ganquan, for example, argues that Chinese heroes, whether of Han (Chinese) decent or from one of the smaller nationalities, should rightfully be considered national heros of contemporary China.[79] In the same vein, a recently published series of articles stresses the "contribution" of the leaders of the independent Dzungar khanate, who, having been defeated by the Chinese army, nevertheless, strove "to strengthen the friendly relationship" between the khanate and the Qing empire. The argument underlying this scenario is that the Qing empire was the "successor" of the formerly independent Dzungar khanate, and that the khanate's subjects willingly became "subjects of China." By characterizing the khanate's leaders as national "heros" of China, the articles also "prove" that these territories wholly belong to the modern Chinese state.

In their articles, the "Short Biography of Gushi-han"[80] Ma Ruheng and Ma Dazheng also adopt the "all heros are Chinese heros" line of argument. They focus on the "contribution" of the Mongolian chief Gushi-han to the "strengthening" of the relationship between the people of Qinghai, Tibet and Mongolia and the Chinese empire. Ma Ruheng in another article, "A Short Writing about Batur-huntaiji -- the Founder of the Dzungars' Political Power"[81] called this chief of the Mongolians "one of the most prominent national leaders in all Chinese history." Ma Ruheng argues against the fact that Batur-huntaiji attempted to protect the independence of his khanate by strengthening his ties with Russia, Ma stresses that Batur-huntaiji maintained ties with the Qing empire in China.[82] Ma Ruheng emphasized that his article is based on many Mongolian archival materials and that his work helps to "correct the arguments of several foreign scholars" who claim that Batur-huntaiji had no relationship with the Qing government. Although he in fact offers no documentary proof, Ma Ruheng

---

[78] Wang Bingzai. "Marriages in the Neolith Era. Comparative Study of the Evenks' Kinship System". *Shixue Jikan*. #3. 1983; Lü Guantian. "Orochens' Social Structures during the Late Qing Dynasty". *Nei Menggu Shehui Kexue*. #5. 1982; Lü Guantian. "Evenks' System of Eight-banners During the Qing Dynasty". *Minzu Yanjiu*. #3. 1983; Zhao Fengcai. "Demographic Development of Orochens". *Minzu Yanjiu*. #2. 1988 and various other articles.

[79] *Guangmin Ribao*. 10.26.1983.

[80] *Minzu Yanjiu*. #2. 1983.

[81] *Xibei Shidi*. #4. 1983.

[82] *Zhongguo Lishi Nianjian*. 1984. P.180-181.

insists that Batur-huntaiji "sent tributary embassies and established an official tributary relationship with the Qing's central government.[83]" Naturally, this "incorporation" of historical heros of Mongolian origin into "Chinese history" in most cases is considered in Mongolia and Russia as attempts to find a historical legacy to disprove current borders and strengthen Chinese influence in these peripheral lands strategically important for both Russia and China to maintain the stability of their borderlands.[84]

Another example of this interpretation of national histories by Chinese scholarship is Cai Jiayi's article "A Short Description of the Commercial Contacts of the Dzungars with the Peoples of the Middle Valley.[85]" Cai points out that commercial contacts between Dzungars and the peoples of China increased dramatically during the reign of Batur-huntaiji and then expanded further during the reigns of Senge, Galdan and Tsevan-Rabdan. These ties peaked during the reign of Galdan-Tseren and his son. According to Cai, two levels of commerce developed: one "official" and the other "private," with both levels influencing political, economic and cultural relations between the Dzungars and Chinese. Cai's argument runs quite contrary to the obvious assertion that the tributary relations which existed sometimes on "official" level between the Central Asian states and China during the 18th and 19th centuries were meant to act as a counterbalance to Russian penetration in the region. And simultaneously any alliance with Russia that existed was to serve as a counterbalance to China's military aggression against the Dzungars though this eventually resulted in the Chinese conquest of the Dzungar khanate.

The history of Kazakhstan has been treated similarly by Chinese scholars. In 1983, Su Beihai published three important articles[86] in which he articulated a Sino-centric view of Kazakh history. Su Beihai's main ar-

---

[83] *Ibid.* P. 90.

[84] See, for example, *Mezhdunarodniye Otnosheniya v Tsentralnoi Azii. Dokumenty i Materialy.* (International Relations in Central Asia. Documents and Materials). Vol. 1-2. Moscow. 1989-1990.

[85] *Qinshi Luncun.* #4. 1983. To compare with Russian concepts see the monograph by A.I. Chernyshov. *Obschestvennoye i Gosudarstvennoye Razvitiye Oiratov v 18 Veke* (The Social and State Development of Oirats in the 18th Century). Moscow. 1990. In this book the Russian-Chinese polemics on the Dzungars history is provided. See also: V.A. Moiseev. "Some problems in the Study of the Relationship between Kazakhs and Oirats in Soviet Historiography". *Voprosi Istoriographii i Istochnikivedeniya Kazakhstana* (Problems of Historiography and Study of Sources in Kazakhstan). Alma-Ata. 1988; Sanchyrov. "History of the Oirats in the 13th - 18th Centuries in the Works of Russian Orientalists during the Pre-Revolutionary Epoch". *Kalmikovedeniye: Voprosi Istoriographii i Bibliographii* (Study on Kalmuks: Problems of Historiography and Bibliography). Elista. 1988.

[86] Su Beihai. "Aggression of Tsarist Russia against Younger Jus of Kazakhs". *Xinjiang Daxue Xuebao.* #1. 1983; Su Beihai. "Aggression of Tsarist Russia against Middle Joos of Kazakhs". Ibid. #2; Su Beihai. "Aggression of Tsarist Russia against Elder Joos of Kazakhs and the Struggle of Peoples against Russia". Ibid. #3.

gument is that the Kazakhs and other nationalities in former China's sphere of "influence" were vassals of Chinese emperors. In arguing this, Su Beihai sets forth the least flexible variant of the "unified Chinese nation" paradigm, wherein all of the nationalities currently living in China or its neighboring states are assumed to be "branches" of the much larger Chinese nation. Keeping with all the variants of the dominant paradigm, Su Beihai denounces the "pretensions" of Tsarist Russia toward "China's territories in Central Asia.[87]"

The motivation behind Su Beihai's argument (and others like his) is simple: to disprove Soviet historiography concerning the Kazakh khanates (Joos), which insists that these khanates voluntarily joined the Russian empire.[88] In attacking Soviet scholarship, however, Su Beihai ends oversimplifying the complicated Central Asian historical process, reducing it simply to a question of "conquest" by one people over another. A similar type of abbreviation appears in Ma Xianneng's article "A Short Description of the Origin and Development of Kazakhs.[89]" Ma Xianneng stresses that in 1860 the Qing government signed the Sino-Russian Treaty of Peking, which was unfavorable to China. He goes on to point out that "in the preceding 100 years, nomadic Kazakhs migrated into the areas of Ili, Chuguchak and Altai... and that they, with other Kazakhs indigenous to these regions, became the "true" representatives of Kazakh nationality in China.[90]" And this is presented by Ma Xianneng as justification for Chinese sovereignty over these lands that now belongs to the newborn Kazakhstan. Like Su Beihai, Ma Xianneng implies that "from the middle of the 1860s, Tsarist Russia expanded decisively into the northwestern regions of China where the Kazakhs had settled. By force of arms, Russia conquered the Kazakhs' territories, forcing the Qing government to sign a series of lopsided treaties, the result of which was to transform Kazakhstan into a colony of Tsarist Russia.[91]"

---

[87] An opposite version of the history of international relations in Central Asia (and of relationship between Russia and China in the region) prevailed in Soviet and Russian historiography. See: B.P. Gurevich. *Mezhdunarodniye Otnosheniya v Tsentralnoi Asii v 17 - Pervoi Polovine 19 Veka* (International Relations in Central Asia in the 17th - First Half of the 19th Century). 2nd edition. Moscow. 1983; V.S. Kuznetsov. *Tsinskaya Imperiya na Rubezhakh Tsentralnoi Azii*. (Qing Empire on the Borders of Central Asia). Novosibirsk. 1983.

[88] For understanding the positions of the Soviet historians see: R.B. Suleimenov. V.A. Moiseev. "Against the Forged History of Kazakhstan". *Problemi Dalnego Vostoka* . #4. 1983. P. 172-179. For the latest innovations of Su Beihai see his article: "Development of the Kazakhs' Economics and Culture during the Reign of the Western Liao Dynasty". *Xinjiang Daxue Xuebao*. #4. 1988.

[89] *Minzuxue Yanjiu*. #3. Beijing. 1982.

[90] *Ibid*. P.66.

[91] *Ibid*. P. 67.

The Soviet response to Su Beihai's work has been highly critical. Besides being criticized for his reductionism, Su is taken to test for his lackadaisical handling of several theoretical categories and questions including those of "ethnicity", "nationality", "nation" and "nation-state", none of which is rigorously defined. Su Beihai is also criticized for sidestepping the ethnogenesis of both the Kazakhs and of the Chinese, the history of Dzungar khanate, the rivalry between the Dzungars (Euleuts) and the Kazakhs and the relationship between the Kazakhs and Russia. For their part Soviet scholars, although correctly rising these questions, have tended to be as primitive and oversimplistic in their own arguments as Su Beihai himself.

In another argument, equally offensive to Soviet scholars, Su Beihai points out that Russia "expropriated" 144,000 sq. km of Chinese territory via the Treaty of Peking (this land was to the south and to the west of Balkhash Lake now within the territories of Kazakhstan), and a further 70,000 sq. km in the Ili Valley by the St. Petersburg treaty, 1881.[92]

Su Beihai's work, while indicative of major trends in Chinese historiography, does not represent all of the country's serious scholarship. In contrast to Su Beihai's anti-Russian reductionist analysis, Wang Jianming's article "Appraisal of Research on the Kazakh's History in the People's Republic of China in the Last Years,[93]" which appeared in 1989, stressed the need to reconsider all these problems in light of the modernization processes occurring in Central Asia. Wang argues that there are several disparate and competing opinions among Chinese scholars regarding such key issues as the origin of the Kazakh nation, the development of Kazakh culture, and its relationship to the Qing empire. Wang Jianmin goes on to identify the seminal articles which have perpetuated China's national historiography, arguing indirectly that these studies have been based on ideological bias rather than historical fact. These articles include: Jiazhongkece's "Several Questions Connected with the History of the Kazakhs in Gansu Province,[94]" Mirza-han's "About the Origin and the Formation of the Kazakh Nationality,[95]" Zhong Xinqi's "The Formation of the Kazakh

---

[92] Su Beihai. **Op. cit.**

[93] *Zhongguoshi Yanjiu Dongtai.* #5. 1989.

[94] *Gansu Minzu Yanjiu.* #3. 1982.

[95] *Xinjiang Shehui Kexue.* #3. 1982.

Nationality,[96]" Jia Hefu, Junisi's "Origin of the Ethnonim "Kazakh",[97]" and the later articles of Su Beihai.[98]

Wang Jianmin's article, despite its attempts of critical description of Chinese ideas, is still heavily influenced by trepidation concerning Russian expansionism. This approach is best illustrated by the following quotation from another article written by Luo Zhiping and Bai Congqing[99]:

"After the death of Khan Tauke, the Kazakh khanate consequently fell into decay... After the North-West was united under the Qing dynasty, Khan Ablai referred to himself as a vassal of the Qing and sent tribute[100]. Once this had transpired, Russia then began to pursue its expansionist plans toward China's Asian territories, swallowing the overwhelming majority of the Kazakhs' lands.[101]"

The same assumption appears in Hu Chenhua's article "The Kyrgyzes of the Northwestern Border Areas of the Motherland.[102]" He repeats the argument regarding Russia's conquest of those "substantial territories to the south and to the west of Lake Balkhash." He insists that the Kyrgyz nationality[103] is intimately tied to the Chinese empire and that the Kyrgyzes are one of the many people of China who have had "close and lasting relations with their Chinese motherland.[104]"

In yet another series of scholarly publications, Chinese researchers attempt to show that Pamir was also a part of "sacred Chinese territory." Examples of these articles include: Huang Shangzhang's "Pamir in the History of our Motherland,"[105] Lu Cunkuan's "The Historical Background of the Sino-Soviet Controversy over Pamir,"[106] Su Beihai's "The Borders of the Two Han Dynasties in Kunlun and Kara-Kunlun Regions, in Xiyu

---

[96] *Xinjiang Shifan Daxue Xuebao*. #1. 1983.

[97] *Ili Shifan Xueyuan Xuebao*. #1. 1986 (In Kazakh language).

[98] *Gansu Minjian Yanjiu*. #2. 1986; *Xinjiang Daxue Xuebao*. #4. 1986.

[99] Luo Zhipin. Bai Cunqing. "The First Attempt to Study the Kazakhs' Law System". *Minzu Yanjiu*. #3. 1988.

[100] Another version of these events is described in a book by R.B. Suleimenov. V.A. Moiseev. *Iz Istorii Kazakhstana XVIII Veka [O Vneshnei i Vnutrennei Politike Ablaya]* (On Kazakhsnan's History of the 18th Century [Ablai's Foreign and Domestic Policy]). Alma-Ata. 1988.

[101] *Ibid.* P. 51.

[102] *Renmin Ribao*. 02.21.1984.

[103] He does not specify whether he is referring to Chinese Kyrgyzs or to the Kyrgyzs of Kyrgyzstan, though it appears from the context that he means both.

[104] *Ibid.*

[105] *Xinjiang Shehui Kexue*. #2. 1982.

[106] *Shehui Kexue Zhanxian*. #3. 1982.

("Western Regions") and in Pamir,[107]" and his "The Territories from Davan up to Kokand,[108]" and "Research on the Borders of Tiaozhi and Tiaozhihai in Central Asia[109]" and Lü Yiran's "The Qing's Government Authority over Pamir.[110]"

The argument of an extensive, all-nationality inclusive Chinese "sphere of influence" is used to explain the history of virtually all Chinese border regions. In their article "An Example of the Administration of the Regions along the Lower Stream of Heilongjiang River and of Sakhalin During the Reign of Emperor Qianlong"[111] Dong Yonggong and Guan Jialu stress "the effectiveness of the Qing government's functions" in the regions along the Heilongjiang (Amur) River and Sakhalin. They point out that indigenous people "Hezhe-Feiyake and Feiyake[112] were longtime settlers along the Heilongjiang and Ussuri Rivers and on Sakhalin and that they had accepted Chinese rule long before the Qing dynasty's reign. At the beginning of the Qing reign, Nurhaqi and his immediate successors further subjugated all these nationalities," destroying all remaining vestiges of local autonomy and wedding them to the Chinese empire.[113]

In another article, "Archeological and Historical Studies of the Area to the East of the Ussuri River,[114]" the Chinese scholar Dong Zhuchen attempts to prove that the whole area east of the Ussuri River historically belonged within "the Chinese sphere of influence." Dong Zhuchen's article is based on the results of archeological diggings, Chinese traditional chronicles, books by Russian and Western travelers, monographs by Soviet scholars published in the Soviet Union during the 1950s (i.e., during the era of the "Great Friendship" between the USSR and China) etc. He, like other Chinese historians, criticizes Russia for attempting to "force" native peoples "to forget their Chinese origin" and especially for replacing local Chinese with Russian geographical names, alien to the region.

The anonymous author of the article "Nationalities of Sakhalin during the Yuan Epoch,[115]" alleges, controversially, that the nationalities living on Sakhalin were conquered by the Mongols in 1308 during the reign of the

---

[107] *Xinjiang Shida Xuebao*. #2. 1982.

[108] *Xinjiang Daxue Xuebao*. #2. 1982.

[109] *Ibid*. ##2-3.

[110] *Shixue Yuekan*. #5. 1992.

[111] *Lishi Dang'an*. #2. 1984.

[112] Small native groups indigenous to these areas.

[113] *Ibid*. P. 88-90.

[114] *Shehui Kexue Zhanxian*. #1. 1984.

[115] *Minzu Yanjiu*. #4. 1989.

Yuan dynasty (1271-1368). The author goes on to analyze the etymology of the peoples living on Sakhalin arguing that the "*iligan*" ethnic group mentioned in Chinese chronicles is, in fact, the Orochen nationality, and that "*guojiaer*" actually refers to the "*nuzhen*" nationality of the Tungusic group.[116] The author claims that the "*iligan*" ethnic group in the Chinese chronicles migrated to Sakhalin from Chinese areas near the Heilongjiang (Amur) River. This assertion is based on archeological diggings which even the author recognizes are not conclusive.[117] The "*gukui*" mentioned in traditional Chinese chronicles are assumed, again controversially, to be the ancestors of the modern Ainu living now in Japan[118] thus indirectly disproving "full Russian legacy" of possessing Sakhalin and from the points of view of some Russian researchers aggravating the Russian-Japanese territorial dispute.

Another relatively independent sub-field is dedicated to the study of Dongbei (Northeast of China), a geographical region consisting of three provinces along the border between China and Russia.[119] Most of the Chinese scholars looking at this area argue that "Dongbei has twice been colonized during the last 100 years, first by Russia and most recently by Japanese imperialism.[120]"

A final example characteristic of current Chinese research in the field of border relations is an article by Xu Guangren and Chen Jinzhong titled "Lin Zexu's Contribution to Building the Defence of Xinjiang.[121]" In this article Xu Guangren and Chen Jinzhong analyze the opinions and works of Gong Ziren, Wei Yuan and Lin Zexu, all scholars and political figures in Qing China recognized as most influential experts on the problems of

---

[116] The "*nuzhen*" nationality is considered by some researchers to be an ancestor of the Manchu people.

[117] *Ibid*. P.98.

[118] *Ibid*. P. 100.

[119] See the monograph by Zhang Boquan. *Dongbei Difang Shigao*. (History of the Chinese Dongbei). Chanchun. 1985; Tian Zhihe. "Reform of Dongbei's Administrative System during the Qing Era". *Dongbei Shida Xuebao*. #4. 1987; *Xiandai Dongbeishi* (Modern History of Dongbei). Jilin. 1986. Russian and Soviet concepts of Dongbei history are the opposite of Chinese. See: *Dalnyi Vostok i Sosednie Territorii v Srednie Veka* (The Far East and Neighboring Territories in the Medieval Times). Novosibirsk. 1980; *Istoriya Severo-Vostochnogo Kitaya. 17 - 20 V.V.* (History of the North-Eastern China in the 17-19th Centuries). Vol.I. Vladivostok. 1987; For a bibliography of the Soviet and Russian literature on the theme see: *Istoriya Manchurii 17-20 V.V. Bibliographicheskyi Ukazatel*. (History of Manchuria in the 17-20th Centuries. Bibliography and Index). Vladivostok. 1981; *Istoriya Severo-Vostoka Kitaya. Bibliographicheskyi Ukazatel*. (History of the North-East of China. Bibliography and Index). Moscow. 1986.

[120] *Dongbei Shida Xuebao*. #3. 1987. P. 96.

[121] *Sichuan Daxue Xuebao*. #1. 1988. The original concept was developed in some earlier works. See: Lin Min. "Lin Zexu's Contribution to the Development of Xinjian's Historical Role". *Xinjiang Shehui Kexue*. #2. 1985; He Ma. "Lin Zexu in Xinjiang". *Fujian Luntan*. #6. 1985. Chen Shenlin. *Lin Zexu yu Yapian Zhanzheng Lungao* (Lin Zexu and the Opium War). Guangzhou. 1985.

China's northern border regions.[122] One of the most questionable points made by the article is the assertion argued by Gong Ziren that massive voluntarily migration from Central China to China's border regions should be a state policy during the Qing reign in rebuffing Russian penetration in the region.[123] Gong Ziren is also supposed to have stressed the necessity of strengthening the Chinese army in the border areas as "a defence against "others"[124] (i.e., Russians), who tried to penetrate Chinese territory through the line of Chinese pickets.[125]" Turning to Wei Yuan, the authors cite one of his major concepts where he argues that "in the reign of Emperor Kangxi,[126] *luocha* (i.e., Russians)[127] robbed people settled in China's east, stealing cattle of the small indigenous ethnic groups, and encouraging escaped Chinese convicts to settle freely in Russian territories adjacent to China, thus challenging the right of the Chinese government to prosecute its vassals.[128] The *luocha* are also accused by Wei Yuan of forcibly halting the payment of tribute by the indigenous ethnic groups to Chinese authorities, and of confiscating land north of the Heilongjiang (Amur) River. Wei Yuan is also supposed by the authors to have emphasized the necessity for the migration of Chinese people to the north to "oppose" Russian expansionism. This policy was pursued by Chinese authorities until now and by some Russian and Central Asian scholars is considered equal to Stalin's policy in the Soviet Union of moving indigenous groups to other places to melt different ethnic groups to keep the empire together. According to Xu Guangren and Chen Jinzhong, the third Qing expert, Lin Zexu, "developed and put into practice" the theoretical opinions of Gong Ziren and Wei Yuan about the necessity "to protect against Russia by strengthening China's northern borders.[129]"

Xu Guangren and Chen Jinzhong analyze the character of Sino-Russian relations in Central Asia as follows:

"The aggressive expansion of Tsarist Russia, regarding the northwestern [sic] regions of China, began in the first half of the 17th century by means

---

[122] All works in that sub-field were analyzed in the book *Zhongguo Lishi Nianjian*, published every year. See, for example, *Zhongguo Lishi Nianjian*. Beijing. 1986. P. 101-102.

[123] *Sichuan Daxue Xuebao*. 1988. P. 78.

[124] This quotation comes from Gong Ziren' work and appears in the Xu Guanren/Chen Jinzhong's article.

[125] *Ibid*. P. 79.

[126] 1662-1722.

[127] The origin of the ethnonym "*luocha*" is in the word "*rakshas*", meaning demon in Sanskrit.

[128] *Ibid*. P. 86.

[129] *Ibid*.

of building a series of towns and lines of fortification in the area of the middle stream of Irtish River. They became the foundation for Russian expansion in the east and the occupation of Kazakhstan's territories in the south. In 1720, Tsarist Russia built the Siberian line of fortification (also known as the Irtish line) between Omsk and Shishankou[130] and from this time, began to pursue aggression along the south bank of the river.

"In the beginning of the 19th century, Russian capitalism began to quickly develop, but the internal market was restrained by the serf system which constituted an obstacle for the freedom of capitalist accumulation. Russia sought not only to reach India through Central Asia in an attempt to gain an exit to the sea in the south, but as well to gain an exit to the sea in the east through Siberia. These exits were seen as essential to enhancing the stable development of Russia's internal market. This was the reason for the Russian annexation of Chinese territories in the northwest and northeast. In 1871, Tsarist Russia invaded Chinese territories to the east and south of Lake Balkhash; built the Saiergaobao[131] fortification between Lake Balkhash and Lake Zaysan to control the routes to Tarbagatai (Tachen); and continuously sent "expeditions" and "research teams" to these regions and as well to Altai to pursue intelligence and expansionist activities. In 1839, Russia created a fishing fleet on Lake Balkhash, seizing considerable fishing areas.

"After the Opium War, Russia began "furtively and quickly" to pursue aggressive activity against the northwestern territories of China, seizing a number of these Chinese territories. Russia quickly began to build a fortification line to southwest of Lake Balkhash, build roads, force the population to migrate, create topographical maps... and insist on opening Russian consulates in Ili, Tachen and Kashgar, etc.[132]"

Xu Guangren and Chen Jinzhong's concluding sentence in this part is equally illustrative:

"All these facts cannot to be unknown to Lin Zexu,[133] and though there are no records made by Lin himself regarding China's defence policy toward Russia, draft versions[134] of reports by General Buyantai to the em-

---

[130] Shishankou (a Pass in the Stone Mountains in Chinese) is now known as Ust-Kammennogorsk and is located in current-day Russia.

[131] Chinese transcription, perhaps, Russian town Sergiopol.

[132] *Ibid.* P. 88-9.

[133] This is a puzzling remark insofar as Lin Zexu lived in the 19th century and was in no way familiar with the interpretation of history current among Chinese scholars.

[134] Never published.

peror, which were co-authored by Lin after his arrival to Ili Valley, indicate the attention he paid to questions of border defence in the northeast.[135]"

The authors also describe the structure of international relations that prevailed in Central Asia after Lin Zexu left the area[136]:

"The sons of Qier (i.e., modern Kazakhs), who were living to the south of the Karatal River, near the Ili River, payed tribute to Russia. During the next year, Russia strengthened Bole[137] and Vernyi,[138] cities to the south of Lake Balkhash, and sent military detachments across the Aksu River which seized Chinese territories south of the Karatal River. In 1847, Russia seized the valleys of the Karatal and Ili Rivers southwest of Lake Balkhash, in the Semirechie area. Thus, the huge territories within the northwestern [sic] borders of China were annexed.[139]"

Xu Guangren and Chen Jinzhong end their article by concluding: "history has confirmed the correctness of Lin Zexu's - the great Chinese patriot of the mid 19th century - attitude regarding the necessity of defence against Russia[140]."

4. NEW CHINESE SCHOLARSHIP

In the late 1980s, a significant shift toward more balance occurred in Chinese historical scholarship. Though still very small, this shift is particularly apparent in articles concerning Sino-Russian relations, the history of border problems and the history of international relations in Central Asia. Many of these revisionist articles have slightly reinterpreted the history of China's changing border. Given the pivotal role played by border questions to the Chinese historiography this is a very important and promising development. Chief among these "new style" historians are Ma Dazheng[141] and Li Dalong,[142] both of whom point out that the study of

---

[135] *Ibid.*

[136] I.e. after 1845.

[137] Chinese transcription.

[138] Modern Almaty, the capital of Kazakhstan.

[139] *Ibid.* P. 90.

[140] *Ibid.*

[141] Ma Dazheng. "Fostering Research on the History of the Formation of Chinese Borders". *Zhongguo Yanjiu Dongtai.* #3. 1989.

China's borders is rooted in ancient and medieval Chinese scholarship. They both regard this field as having a scholarly basis which is independent of the changes that have occurred within 20th century China thus implying the necessity to look at current Chinese borders as a given fact that cannot be disproved. In one of his most recent articles, Ma Dazheng analyzes the scholarly literature of the Guomindang period,[143] stressing the following points, all of which can be considered as indicative of new trends in the Chinese historiography:

- changes of China's borders during recent times;
- distinctions between the border policies of China's various dynasties;
- and, history of the formation of China's borders[144].

Ma Dazheng further subdivides these into the following topics of research:

- China's border policy during different epochs and the changing structure of border authorities;
- both the essence and the constituent parts of China's various border policies;
- history of the different nationalities living either currently or previously within the border territories;
- ideological basis of the various border policies;
- interrelationship between political, national, military, economic and cultural concerns and China's border problems;
- and the interrelationship between people, historical events, geographical areas and China's border problems.[145]

Much like his colleague Ma Dazheng, Li Dalong calls for a historical reconsideration of the Qing period (1644-1911) when the current Sino-Russian border was formed. This border between Russia, the newly independent Central Asian states and China remains virtually unchanged from the late 19th century. Li Dalong's new research agenda draws attention to the following points:

---

[142] Li Dalong. "About the Academic Congress on the History of the Formation of Chinese Borders". *Minzu Yanjiu.* #3. 1989.
[143] Ma Dazheng. **Op. cit.** P. 21.
[144] *Ibid.* P.18.
[145] *Ibid.* P.19.

- border policy during the Qing era;
- Qing policy toward Tibet;
- Qing policy toward Xinjiang;
- Qing border defence policy.[146]

Ma Dazheng and Li Dalong's agendas illustrate the changes occurring in the Chinese social sciences toward more balanced research. Their frameworks are based less on ideological considerations and more on the process of historical change. Research undertaken this way will be more internally oriented[147] and less concerned with justifying a large, expansionist China. The Chinese historiography in the 1990s is also encouraging the use of different types of sources. As a result, the spectrum of scholarly opinion is being broadened and new hypotheses are being presented. The only point of hesitation regarding this new revisionism is that to date the inconclusive shift is mostly confined to specialized works on narrow scholarly questions. It's impact on the Chinese mainstream historiography is still to come.

B. Chinese Scholars on the History of Sino-Russian Relations and the History of the Formation of Sino-Russian Border

1. Sino-Russian Relations and the Formation of the Border

Those questions related to Sino-Russian relations were elaborated upon in detail in the articles concerning more narrow, specialized fields, such as the history of Sino-Russian relations or the history of frontier problems. In 1983, an article by Zhou Shengde "History Cannot be Forged; About the Book "*Sino-Russian Relations in the 17th Century. Volume I*" " was published in the first issue of the journal *Studies of the USSR and Eastern Europe*.[148] Zhou analyzed the usefulness of Russian archival materials from the point of view of current Chinese historical concepts and come to the very con-

---

[146] *Minzu Yanjiu.* P. 75.

[147] This orientation helped to make possible Sino-Russian border normalization in the 1990s.

[148] *Sulian Dong'ou Yanjiu.* #1. 1983. P. 93.

troversial conclusion that scholars should rely only on Chinese documents.

In the article, Russian policy in the region is traditionally painted in very dark colors: Russian pioneers-Cossacks like Khabarov and Poyarkov were called not only "the Russian conquistadors of the 17th century," but also "the conductors of the expansionist plans... of Tsarist Russia in the Far East," and "according to the testimony of native peoples, - cannibals.[149]" Zhou Shengde stresses that in indigenous groups Cossacks still revive the images of "tortures, sufferings... [and] deaths.[150]"

Chinese scholars continued publications on specific Sino-Russian frontier problems in the mid-to-late 1980s.[151] For example, an valuative article by Bu Ping "The Studies Concerned with the Eastern Sector[152] of the Russo-Chinese border" was published in 1983.[153] The thesis of this article is focused on attempts to prove that the border in this portion of the Sino-Russian frontier was historically formed in the 17th century and experienced considerable changes in the 19th century due to the "expansionist policy" of Tsarist Russia. Bu Ping stresses that these changes have been maintained up to the present day. According to Bu Ping's assertion, that "to prove that the formation of the frontier was reasonable, we should first look if past treaties recognize the traditional frontiers of the administrative jurisdiction of both sides and whether the treaty maintains this traditional jurisdiction" in its provisions.[154] The Chinese author points out that the Treaty of Nerchinsk, favorable to China, "maintains the traditional boundaries [of the Chinese empire]." Consequently, it is Bu Ping's opinion that only this early Sino-Russian treaty signed in the atmosphere of the clear dominance of the Chinese empire in the region can define the current Russo-Chinese border according to "the principle of justice." The author writes:

---

[149] *Ibid.* P. 94.

[150] *Ibid.*

[151] See, for example: Guan Peiwei. "It is not Easy to Misrepresent the History of the Sino-Soviet Border Formation". *Qushi Xuekan.* #5. 1982; Shao Yan. "Short Appraisal of the Book *The History of the Formation of the Borders of North-West of China*". *Shehui Kexue Zhanxian.* #1. 1983; Su Beihai. "The Sino-Russian Kashgar Agreement of 1934 and the Border Question." *Xinjiang Shifan Daxue Xuebao.* #2. 1983; "The Chinese Ownership over the Territories Around the Baikal Lake and the Basin of the Heilongjiang River during Liao and Jin Dynasties". *Xuexi yu Tansuo.* #3. 1984; Lü Banghou. "The Discussion about the Ploughed Boundary-strip Near the 64 Villages, situated to the East of the River and the Events on the Ploughed Land of Su Zhong'a". *Shehui Kexue Zhanxian.* #2. 1985.

[152] The Eastern sector is the Central Asian portion of the former Sino-Soviet border. Western sector is the portion of the border in the Far East.

[153] *Xuexi yu Tansuo.* #6. 1983.

[154] *Ibid.* P. 125.

"In its territorial expansion, Russia [in the 17th century] had reached only the basin of the Lena River, and therefore had no contacts with traditional Chinese boundaries. Moreover, Russia had no adequate understanding of the real situation in the area. It was under these circumstances that China established its sovereignty over the whole of the Hailongjiang [Amur] River Basin,[155] which had no relations with Russia. In the mid-17th century when the Russians violated these traditional Chinese boundaries [in the Heilongjiang region], the Qing government launched a strong attack against the Russian military detachments, proving its readiness to maintain the border.[156]"

The Chinese author believes that within the Eastern (Central Asian) sector of the border, the degree of preciseness concerning the borderline was less than in the Western sector, and this fact explains why "the drawing of the border line on maps diverged from the reality of the situation."[157]

In the second section of his article Bu Ping tries to develop his idea, emphasizing the fact that in the 19th century "Russia seized a huge portion of the Chinese territories, and as the result of this process the border of the 18th century, which had been kept for more than 150 years and had played a significant role, had been changed by the reality of the 19th century."[158] According to Bu Ping, the main feature of the 19th century border was characterized by a "violent division of the territories," and because of that, this border, which was formed under the Treaties of Aigun and Peking, "was unjust and unreasonable." Bu Ping writes:

"These two [Aigun and Peking] treaties, were unequal; they were concluded under circumstances when the strong power, Russia, according to its economic needs and relying on its political and military supremacy, forced the weak party, China, which was suffering from both external and internal difficulties, to consent with the unjust drawing of the borders.

Thus China was forced to leave the regions which were under its jurisdiction. This process led to territorial changes on a great scale."[159]

---

[155] I.e. also to the part of Amur basin which is within current Russian borders.

[156] Ibid. P. 126.

[157] The concepts by Bu Ping were further elaborated in his articles: "The Formation of the Western Part of the Eastern Sector of the Sino-Russian Border". *Zhongguo Bianjiang Shidi Yanjiu Baogao*. #1. 1987. Unfortunately this journal is for the internal use and legally is not accessible by the foreign researchers. For an analysis of the information in the Chinese maps see the article: Lu Yuantu. "General Approach to the Maps of the Early Period of the Eastern Part of the Sino-Russian Border". *Sulian Dong'ou Guojia Yanjiu*. (Study of the USSR and Eastern Europe). Vol. 1,2. Beijing. 1988.

[158] *Xuexi yu Tansuo*. P. 127-128.

[159] Ibid. P. 128.

According to the author's opinion, two reasons can explain the unjust and unrational character of the border in the 19th century:

1. "In the new Russian territories, the leading role was still played by the Chinese people,"[160]
2. "In general -- in both political aspects and in economics ones -- all facts prove that the south and the north of Heilongjiang (i.e., the territories both to the south and the north of the Heilongjiang [Amur] River) were one inseparable part," and Tsarist Russia "tore out these traditional stable ties."[161]

The author then attempts to explain in detail why the frontier of the 19th century has been kept up to the 20th century. It is Bu Ping's opinion that this occurred "not because Russia was satisfied with the frontier"[162] but can be attributed to three reasons:

1. A new international situation has emerged: an eight-nation expeditionary force invasion of China "bounded Russia's feet and hands."
2. The Russian working class awoke and "fixed the Russian tsarist government."
3. The Tsarist government was concerned that "Siberia would be completely inhabited by non-Russian people."[163]

An article by Fu Sunming, "The Primary Course of the Relationship Between Russia and China in the 18th century," which further developed these ideas, was published in 1984.[164] In this article, Fu Sunming tries to elaborate on his concept of Russian foreign policy in the 18th century and during the entirety of the Russian state's existence. The main premise of this concept is that after the death of Peter the Great, Russia "pursued a policy of global aggression.[165]" To strengthen this idea, the Chinese author uses all possible and impossible facts, including false "testament" of Peter the Great as reliable historical argument. Relying on such characterizations of Russian foreign policy, Fu Sunming tries to analyze Russo-

---

[160] *Ibid.* P.130
[161] *Ibid.*
[162] *Ibid.* P. 131.
[163] *Ibid.*
[164] *Dongbei Shida Xuebao.* #2. 1984.
[165] *Ibid.* P. 50.

Chinese relations, stressing at first the leading premise of his concept: "The main goal of Russia in its trade with China was not to keep the commercial balance between import and export, but simply to extract gold and silver from China."[166]

The author then analyses the history of the Sino-Russian relations in the 18th century. His conclusion is the following:

> "On the one hand Russia reaped huge profits from its commerce with China, and on the second - provoked incidents in the northern part of Mongolia[167], which belongs to China, and along the northwestern part of the [Sino-Russian] border to complicate the relations with China... The process of the development of Russian capitalism in the 18th century was the realization of its global-scale aggressive policies. The characterizing trend of Russian policies toward China was the use of its commerce with China for the development of the Russian capitalist economy for the benefit of the Russian expansionist... foreign policy."[168]

In 1984 in the journal *Study of Modern History* Xue Xiantian and Li Jiagu published the article "Concerning the Character of Sino-Russian Relations in Modern Times; An Answer to Narochnitskyi and Tikhvinskyi.[169,170]" According to the author's notions, "the most typical events, reflecting the essence of relations between China and Russia, were the events which occurred during a period which began in the mid 19th century, when Tsarist Russia forced China to conclude a series of unequal treaties."[171] The first of these unequal treaties, which were forced by Russia was the "Treaty of Commerce in Kuldja and Chuguchak, Concluded Between Russia and China on July 25, 1851," a purely commercial treaty, which is considered by Chinese scholars as similarly unequal for China as the Treaty of Nanking between China and Great Britain, under which Britain received the rights of consular jurisdiction within China according which British citizens who committed crimes on Chinese territories must be judged by British court and by the British laws.

---

[166] *Ibid.* P. 51.

[167] Now the Republic of Mongolia.

[168] *Ibid.* P. 52.

[169] A.L.Narochnitskyi and S.L. Tikhvinskyi, most renown Soviet historians (both have Ambassadorial ranks and are full members of the Soviet Academy of Sciences) were the highest ranked Soviet historians who ever wrote on the history of the Sino-Russian and Sino-Soviet relations. They edited practically all books on the history of Russian foreign policy and the history of Sino-Russian relations published in the Soviet Union in the 1960's, 1970's and 1980's.

[170] *Jindaishi Yanjiu.* #4. 1984.

[171] *Ibid.* P. 233.

Xue Xiantian and Li Jiagu also emphasize that from the end of the 1850s and up to the beginning of the 1860s, Tsarist Russia forced China to conclude such unequal treaties as the Treaty of Aigun, of Tientsin, of Peking, etc. These Chinese authors have stressed the fact that "in 1781, Russia had begun the colonial war for the conquest of the Ili valley," and, had "openly seized this region by military means." According to this Chinese notion:

> "Russian colonial dominance in the region lasted for ten years. Finally, at the end of that period, Russia forced China to conclude another unequal treaty - the so-called Changed Treaty.[172] Under this treaty, and five following protocols, Russia has seized a considerable part of Chinese territories[173] and received as tribute five million [and] ninety thousand silver *liangs* [taels] from China."[174]

In this article all Sino-Russian treaties, as usually excluding the Treaty of Nerchinsk and the Treaty of Burinsk, are considered as being similar to unequal treaties concluded with China by Great Britain and France in the 19th century, thus disproving the historical legacy of the former Sino-Soviet borders. The authors stress that all such treaties between China and the Western powers (whether that power be Great Britain, France or Russia), "were unwieldy chains forced upon the Chinese people, and [that] all such treaties are incontestable proof of the colonial robbery and aggression of these states."[175] Relying upon this appraisal of Russian foreign policy toward China in the 19th century, the researchers attempt to analyze more distant periods of time, emphasizing that even in the 1640s, the Tsarist government "often sent heavily armed detachments of Cossacks to invade the Heilongjiang area,[176] which belongs to China, and the territories east of Lake Baikal to fulfill the aggressive will of the Russian nobility and the new class of merchants."[177] Thus the early history of Sino-Russian relations in the estimation of the authors is "the history of the Russian military invasion of the border regions of eastern China, and the history of the military struggle of the Chinese people against the aggression of the

---

[172] Also called the Ili or St. Petersburg Treaty.

[173] The same appraisal of the Treaty can be seen in another Chinese article: "Black Water, White Mountains: about People and Society. The Foreword to the New Book by Huan Weihan *Heishui Xianminzhuan* (History of the Peoples who Lived near Heilongjiang)". *Shehui Kexue Zhanxian*. #2. 1985.

[174] *Jindaishi Yanjiu*. #4. 1984. P.286.

[175] *Ibid*. P. 287.

[176] By Heilongjiang in this case the authors mean the territories to the North of the Heilongjiang River.

[177] *Ibid*. P. 287.

Tsarist Russia."[178] The authors presented Russian foreign policy in the same light during the Second Opium War.

The book, written by another researcher - Zhou Weizhou - *A Short Historical Survey of the Aggression of Great Britain and Russia Toward our Tibet* appeared in 1984.[179] In this book, Zhou Weizhou -- "basing [his research] on a large amount of historical materials," (mostly Chinese) -- attempts to show "how the imperialist powers, Great Britain and Russia, developed plans to conquer Chinese Tibet."[180] Zhou Weizhou holds the opinion that Russia in the 19th-to-early 20th centuries, under the pretext to pursue ethnographic research and to study Buddhism, not only penetrated Tibet with the intention of pursuing its own underground activity, but also attempted to utilize a group within the Tibetan ruling circle to reorient the country toward Russia. In the fourth chapter of the book, entitled "Russian Underground Activities to Conquer Tibet" all Russian explorers and scholars who were in Tibet at the time are considered by the author as "spies," who pursued unlawful activities against China.[181] In the spring of 1985 Xi Boshi published a review of Zhou Weizhou's book. In this review he stressed that the monograph by Zhou Weizhou "systematically describes the history of aggression of English and Russian imperialism up to 1919 toward the southwestern frontiers of China."[182]

Another book, *Tsarist Russia and Dongbei*,[183] published in Chanchun in 1985, analyzes the policy of the Qing government "to rebuff the Russian aggression" between 1643 and 1917.[184] The main premise of the book is that "Tsarist Russia was a European state which had no frontiers with China" and that "the persistent expansion of this state toward the East," forced China to establish the border with Russia.[185] The entire history of relations between the Russian and Chinese people is considered in this book through "the aggressive character" of Russian foreign policy toward

---

[178] *Ibid*. P. 292-3.

[179] Zhou Weizhou. *Ying E Qinlüe Woguo Xizang Shilüe* (Short Historical Description of the British and Russian Aggression toward owr Tibet). Xian. 1984.

[180] *Ibid*. P. 3. See also P. 4,5.

[181] Russian historiography found different explanation of these events. See, for example, S. N. Goncharenko "The Exchange of Diplomatic Letters with Zongliyamen about the Przhevalskyi Request to Travel through Central Asia". *22th Academic Conference "State and Society in China"*. Vol. 1. Moscow. 1991; L.L. Zarutskaya "Chinese Official Thanks Russian Travellor". *Ibid*. Vol. 3; N.S. Kuleshov. "Russia and Tibet in 1900-1914". *Tsybykovskiye Chteniya*. Ulan-Ude. 1989.

[182] *Guangming Ribao*. 3.04.1985.

[183] The North-East of China.

[184] *Sha E yu Dongbei* (Tsarist Russia and the North-East). Ed. by Tong Dong. Changchun. 1985.

[185] *Ibid*. P. 667.

China. According to the Chinese authors, the essence of the history of Sino-Russian relations consisted of "Russian aggression" and, "the rebuff to this aggression by the native population."[186] The entire history of relations between Russian and Chinese in this book is considered from this angle.

If these recent publications are to be spoken of, then the Chinese textbook, *General Information about the Soviet Union*,[187] should be considered. In this book, one can find a general appraisal of Russian foreign policy toward China. The prominent professors of eleven leading universities and pedagogical institutes of primary Chinese cities took part in the preparation of this textbook for the Russian departments of universities all over the country. The second segment of this book is dedicated to a short history of Russia and the Soviet state. The most interesting are three chapters: "From Kievan Russia (*Kievskaya Rus*) to Russia of the 17th century," "Russia in the 18th century" and, "Russia in the 19th century." The main historical concept advocated by the textbook is epitomized by the implications of "expansionist wars" waged by Russia upon China's historical development. These wars, according to the authors, constitute the dominant trait of the policies exercised toward its neighbors by Russia's ruling classes during disparate periods. The Chinese authors portray Russian foreign policy in a very unflattering (to say the least) light; especially foreign policy following the period of Ivan IV's reign. The entire history of the conquest of Siberia, from the reign of Boris Godunov, is seen as a persistent Russian seizure of Chinese territories.

In this textbook an appraisal of the policy of Peter the Great intrinsic to the Chinese historiography of the 1980s and early 1990s is quite apparent to the reader:

> "Pursuing consistent aggressive wars, Peter I not only transformed continental Russia into a sea power, but also elaborated ambitious plans for an external expansion to achieve global hegemony for Russian Empire."[188]

According to the authors' notion, "the external expansion of Tsarist Russia," during the rule of Catherine II, "developed into large-scale aggression."[189] The authors of the textbook write that "the struggle for world

---

[186] *Ibid.* P. 1.

[187] *Sulian Jikuang* (General Information about the Soviet Union). Ed. by Li Mingbing. Beijing. 1986.

[188] *Ibid.* P. 155.

[189] *Ibid.* 159.

hegemony require the territorial expansions which are persistent trends in Russian foreign policy" during the 19th century.

The authors then develop the idea that after being defeated in the Crimea War, Tsarist Russia reasserted its expansion into Asia, and by taking advantage of the military aggression of the European powers toward China, "forced the Qing government to sign a series of unequal treaties.[190]" The authors stress:

> "Taking advantage of the militarist aggression of the British and French armies against China, Tsarist Russia forced the Qing government to sign the asymmetric Sino-Russian Treaty of Aigun in 1856 and Sino-Russian Treaty of Peking in 1860, seizing more than one million sq. km of Chinese territory north of Heilongjiang, south of the External Khingan Mountains[191], and west of the Ussuri River including Sakhalin. In 1864, Russia forced the Qing government to sign the unequal Protocol of the Demarcation of the Northwestern Borders between Russia and China, and included by force, 440 thousand sq.km of the territory within western China. Then, according to the unequal Sino-Russian Ili Treaty (1881) and several subsequent protocols demarcating the borders, Tsarist Russia seized in addition more then 70 thousand sq. km of the territory in the western part of China. Thus, in less than half a century, Russia seized 1.5 million sq. km of Chinese territory."[192]

These examples do not illustrate fully the entire content of the chapter, in which the history of the Russian state is analyzed, but they do epitomize the conceptual core of the historical section of the book.

An article written by Qin Hepin, "An Analysis of the Historical Background of the Signing the Sino-Russian Treaty of Ili by Zeng Jize," is dedicated to the Chinese analysis of the Treaty of Ili (the Treaty of St. Petersburg).[193] After a brief Chinese traditional description of international relations in the Central Asia up to 1871 and the diplomatic atmosphere in which the Sino-Russian Treaty of Livadia was concluded, the Chinese researcher comes to the conclusion that "Chun Hou[194] gave in to Russian pressure and seduction," and signed the Treaty of Livadia, "violating in-

---

[190] *Ibid.* 187.

[191] The Chinese name of Russian Stanovoy Khrebet. Generally Stanovoy and a part of Yablonovoy Khrebet were called in China External Khingan, and current Greater and Lesser Khingan ranges as Interior Khingan.

[192] *Ibid.*

[193] *Chengdu Daxue Xuebao.* #4. 1985. Reprinted in: *Zhongguo Jindaishi Baokan Ziliao Xuanhui.* #3. 1986.

[194] The Qing's representative during the Sino-Russian negotiations in 1879.

structions of the Qing government."[195] This unproven fact, according to Qin Hepin, was the Qing government's precise reason for "calling Chun Hou back," and "insisting on the conclusion of a new treaty."[196]

The article describes the Chinese stance on Russian reasons for sending military detachments to the Ili Valley; analyzes the views of the new Qing's envoy to Russia, Zeng Jize, who was appointed after Chun Hou; and on the possible development of the situation in the region.[197] At the end the Chinese author, contrary to the dominant Chinese paradigm, shows quite correctly "the clear divergences between different strata of the Russian ruling circles on expansion in Central Asia"[198] and stresses that the Russian military establishment insisted on escalation of the conflict, but this position was not supported by diplomats and financial circles.[199] The author also analyzes the attitude of Great Britain, France and Germany toward the Ili issue and makes the unusual (for Chinese historical science) conclusion that external forces must affect the Russian foreign policy.[200] According to the author's opinion only these prerequisites allowed Zeng Jize to sign the Treaty of Ili and to return the Ili Valley to China.[201]

Another Chinese book on the theme, authored by Kong Jingwei and Zhu Xianpin, entitled *The Economic Robbery of the Region of Harbin by Imperialist Russia* was published in August 1986.[202] The main goal of the book is to show the Russian Far East's economic dependence on China. According to the author, both the population's and the military detachment's food supply in the Russian Far East was imported mostly from northwestern and northeastern China. This is why, according to Kong Jingwei and Zhu Xianpin, that northwestern and northeastern China, and especially the region of Harbin, was "the main subject of the robbery from im-

---

[195] *Ibid.* P.69.

[196] *Ibid.*

[197] For a detailed explanation of these events based on a comparison of Chinese and Russian archival materials—see my forthcoming book *The Sino-Russian St. Petersburg Treaty of 1881: Diplomatic History*.

[198] *Ibid.* P. 70.

[199] *Ibid.* P. 70-71.

[200] *Ibid.* P.73.

[201] For another explanation of these events see my articles "Zeng Jize - Diplomat, Scholar, Litterati of the New Time". *20th Academic Conference "State and Society in China"*. Vol. 2. Moscow. 1989; "Instructions for the Qing Representative Zeng Jize at the Sino-Russian Negotiations in 1880-1881 in St.Petersburg and the History of One Forged Document". *21 Academic Conference "State and Society in China"*. Vol. 2. Moscow. 1990. See also the bibliography to my forthcoming book *The Sino-Russian St.Petersburg Treaty of 1881: Diplomatic History*..

[202] Kong Jingwei, Zhu Xianpin. Di E Dui Haerbin Idaidi Jingji Jingduo. (The Economic Robbery of the Region of Harbin by Imperialist Russia). Harbin. 1986.

perialist Russia."[203] It should be stressed that large amounts of statistical material and different spreadsheets were supplied by the authors to prove their point—they tried to use not very well known primary sources on the economic history of China but failed to do it academically correctly. The Chinese authors especially stressed in the article's conclusion that Russian "aggressive" foreign policy was transformed into course benevolent to China when the representatives of "the socialist USSR" replaced the representatives of the old Russia.[204]

The book, *The History of the Aggression of Tsarist Russia against China*, was published at the end of 1986.[205] In the foreword the authors stress that the book was written in the 1970s. Then after several copies were published, the initial text was enlarged, rewritten and the first "official" edition appeared in October 1986. The first and the second sections of the book are dedicated to the authors' "original" idea of "Russian state expansion." According to this concept Russian expansion was stopped in the 16th century on the frontier defined by "the Enisei River, the upper part of Lena River, and Lake Baikal"[206] and these geographical frontiers marked the Russian borders in Siberia. The Chinese scholars accuse the Russian government of resorting to a variety of "deceptive plans for achieving its own avaricious goals." Thus, even the anti-Manchu rebellion of the so-called three feudatories (known in Chinese history as "Sanfan rebellion"), which followed the Manchu conquest of China in the 17th century, was "used" by Russia to "seize Chinese territories in the basin of the Heilonjiang (Amur) River." The authors' notion holds that the Taiping uprising was also used by the tsar's diplomats to force China into signing "unequal treaties."[207]

---

[203] Ibid. P.7. For the Russian version of the events see: G.N. Romanova. *Ekonomicheskie Otnosheniya Rossii i Kitaya na Dalnem Vostoke [19 - Nach.20 V.]*. (Economic relations of Russia and China in the Far East [19th - Early 20th Century]). Moscow. 1987; G.N. Romanova. "The Meaning of the Russian-Chinese Trade Ties in Colonizing the Far East". *Khozyaistvennoye Osvoeniye Russkogo Dalnego Vostoka v Epokhu Kapitalizma*.(Colonizing the Russian Far East in the Epoch of Capitalism). Vladivostok. 1989.

[204] Ibid. P. 90.

[205] *Sha E Qin Hua Shi* (The History of the Aggression of the Tsarist Russia against China). Ed. by Mo Yongming. Shanghai. 1986.

[206] Ibid. P. 4.

[207] Opposite Russian views on this problem are discussed in: A.A. Brezhnev. "The Intervention of the Western Powers against Taipings and Russian Public Opinion". *12th Academic Conference "State and Society in China"*. Vol. 2. Moscow. 1981; A.A. Brezhnev. "Russia and the Taipings' Peasant War". *Dokumenty Opprovergayut. Protiv Falsifikatsii Istorii Russko-Kitaiiskikh Otnosheniyi* (Documents Refute. Against Falsification of History of the Russian-Chinese Relations). Moscow. 1982. See also an English version of this book: *Chapters from the History of Russo-Chinese Relations, 17th - 19th Centuries*. Moscow. 1985.

In this book, the expeditions of Russian pioneers-Cossacks Khabarov, Poyarkov, etc... to Siberia are considered as being only simple military campaigns aimed at the seizure of foreign (Chinese) territories, and any acts of the violence committed by Russians toward the native populations are strongly stressed. In the authors' own language, these expeditions were "the first cases of Russian aggression toward Chinese lands, which eventually brought innumerable suffering to the native population."[208]

All Sino-Russian treaties in the book are regarded as unequal; even the Treaty of Nerchinsk -- despite the fact that when signed, the Manchu Empire was exerting considerable pressure upon the incompetent Russian envoy -- is shown by the authors as yielding certain unfair rewards to Russia.[209]

The process of Russo-Chinese border formation in Central Asia is also described in the book in great detail. This process has been regarded by Chinese scholars as unjust and unequal, and consequently the Treaty of Peking, the Chuguchak Protocol and the Treaty of St. Petersburg are considered as having been imposed upon China under the threat of Russian military force. For example, after analyzing the articles of the Treaty of St. Petersburg and stressing that by signing this treaty, the Chinese envoy Zeng Jize had managed to obtain for China considerable concessions from the Russians compared with the (nonratified by the Chinese) Treaty of Livadia, the authors still considered even the establishing of Russian consulates[210] in China as an act of pressure from the Russian government.[211]

An exclusive section of the book has been reserved for the question of Pamir.[212] The border agreement concerning the Pamirs between Russia and China is considered by the Chinese authors as a "conspiracy between Russia and Great Britain to divide Pamir among them." Pamir, as well as Tibet, in the authors' view, was "always a subordinate Chinese territory."[213]

Within the book, the Chinese concept of "Russian aggressive foreign policy" is described rather thoroughly. The researchers attempt to prove that "the abnormal development of capitalism in Russia and the remnants of the serf system" lead to the narrowness of the internal economic field,

---

[208] *Sha E Qin Hua Shi*. P. 25-26.

[209] *Ibid*. P. 41-53.

[210] Article 10 of the St. Petersburg Treaty of 1881.

[211] For the detailed description of Russian-Chinese polemics over establishing Russian consulates in China see my forthcoming book *The Sino-Russian St.Petersburg Treaty of 1881: Diplomatic History*..

[212] *Sha E Qin Hua Shi*. P. 207-223.

[213] *Ibid*. P. 207.

and thus to the search of external markets. In the authors' view, these facts give rise to some very serious implications concerning Russian foreign policy. In the authors' interpretation of history, "the Russian expansionist course" parallels Western, and especially Japanese, foreign policies.

The book analyzes "the history of Russian aggression toward China" up to 1917. The tsarist government is accused of not only planning "to seize and divide" Tibet between Russia and Great Britain, but of " attempts" to suppress the Republican revolution of 1911 (The *Xinhai* revolution).[214] The signing of the agreement which provided for the autonomy of Outer Mongolia is understood by the Chinese authors as an attempt by tsarist diplomats to impose their control over Mongolia - if not by seizing it than at least by making "this part of the Chinese territory,"[215] dependent upon Russia.

In the last paragraph of the book the authors stress that "the Great October revolution announced the elimination of this aggressive Russian policy toward China."[216] The authors emphasize the fact that "the October Revolution of 1917, led by Lenin, overthrew the dictatorial regime and buried the imperialist state of Tsarist Russia... thus bringing to an end [to] the Russian tsars' ridiculous hope of forming a world empire."[217] These words were written when the Chinese researchers thought that the Soviet Union would not fell apart and will remain as China still is—a Communist state.

It is necessary to point out that as the 1980s drew to a close, Chinese historiography experienced a shift away from such simplistic historical ideas. For example, Chinese scholars began to bring to a halt the practice of artificially emphasizing the beneficial character of Sino-Russian commerce to Russia. The scholar Wang Shaoping, in his article "Sino-Russian Trade in Xinjiang,[218]" examined the reasons for opening Sino-Russian

---

[214] *Ibid.* P. 400-413.

[215] *Ibid.* P. 438-453. For Russian version of the events see: Ye.A. Belov. "The Position of Russia and China on Mongolia after Proclaiming its Independence [1911-1912]". *22th Academic Conference "State and Society of China".* Vol. 2. Moscow. 1991; I.Yu. Vanina. Yu.V. Kuzmin "The Liquidation of the Qing's Domination in Mongolia and the Public Opinion in Russia". Ibid; S.G. Luzyanin. "The Position of Russia During Chinese Expansion in Mongolia in 1911-1912". *Vzaimootnosheniya Rossii so Stranami Vostoka v Ser. 19 - Nach. 20 V.V..* [sic] (Interactions of Russia with the Oriental Countries in Mid-19th - Beginning of 20th Century). Irkutsk. 1982; S.G. Luzyanin."The Strengthening of the Chinese Positions and Russian Politics in Outer Mongolia [1915-1917]". *Rossiya i Strani Aziatsko-Tikhookeanskogo Regiona v 19 - Nach. 20 V.V.* (Russia and the Countries of the Asian-Pacific Region in the 19th - Early 20th Centuries). Irkutsk. 1988.

[216] *Ibid.* P. 470-474.

[217] *Ibid.* P.474.

[218] *Shixue Jikan.* #4. 1989. For the Russian version of the events see: N.A. Aldabekova "About Russian Trade in Xinjiang from the end of 18th - the '40s of 19th Century". *18th Academic Conference "State and Society in*

trade in the region. He studied, in particular: the initial stage of trade (beginning in 1728), the period lasting from 1851 to 1880, and the period after the Treaty of Ili (1881) until 1914. And though the author has come to the conclusion that Sino-Russian commerce in Xinjiang has not been beneficial for the Chinese side "in view of direct financial profits," nevertheless he stresses that this fact alone, cannot constitute a reason for "neglecting" this commerce. Sino-Russian trade in Xinjiang, in Wang Shaoping's opinion, was in general beneficial for China[219] as the people of Xinjiang received goods, necessary for normal life. This trade aided in the development of agriculture, and China received a considerable sum of money from Russia and thus could increase its stock of hard currency.[220]

Wang Shaoping writes:

"Sino-Russian trade in Xinjiang was pivotal in the strengthening of friendly contacts between the peoples of the two states, especially, those who lived in the Central Asian parts of Russia and China and have the consanguineous ties... This trade created the basis for the development of economic and cultural ties between the Russian and Chinese people, and quickened the development of trade between the USSR and Xinjiang after the October Revolution. In this way, Sino-Russian trade in Xinjiang has made a direct impact on the quick emergence of trade relations between China and the Soviet Union."[221]

2. CURRENT CONCEPTUAL INNOVATIONS AND THE CHINESE SURVEY OF THEIR OWN CONCEPTS

Two articles which analyzed the results of the Chinese research on the ties of China with foreign countries in modern times were published in 1989. In the section dedicated to the history of Sino-Russian and Sino-Soviet relations the Chinese researcher Lu Shuyong stressed:

China". Vol. 2. Moscow. 1987; N.A. Aldabekova "Russian-Chinese Trade in Xinjiang in Mid-19th Century". *Izvestiya AN Kaz.SSR* (Newsletter of the Academy of Science of Kaz.SSSR). #3. Alma-Ata. 1989. J.K. Kasymbaev. Russian Trade with the Qing's Empire through the Cities of Eastern Turkestan (up to Mid-19th Century). *16th Academic Conference "State and Society of China"*. Vol. 2. Moscow. 1985; J.K. Kasymbaev. "Russian Trade Ties with Xinjiang through Eastern Turkestan in the End of 19th - Beginning of 20th Centuries". *13th Academic Conference "State and Society in China"*. Vol. 3. Moscow. 1982 etc.

[219] *Shixue Jikan*. P. 65.
[220] *Ibid*.
[221] *Ibid*. P.66.

"After creating the People's Republic of China, Chinese historians were not paying much attention to the study of the history of Sino-Russian relations. From the 1960s, some Soviet historians meeting the political demands of the Soviet government, published many articles in which they misrepresented the history of the aggression of Tsarist Russia in China. They began to defend openly the aggressive course of Tsarist Russia toward the Chinese territories, and that was the reason for the Chinese to study thoroughly the history of Sino-Russian relations—to clear up the historical facts.

"During 1964-1972 Chinese historians collected a large amount of historical materials, making a wide preparatory work for studying the history of Sino-Russian relations. In the next four years they published a series of articles on the aggression of Tsarist Russia toward the Chinese territories. In these articles they exposed the erroneous ideas of Soviet historians. Based on real historical facts, Chinese historians described correctly the following concepts: the basins of the Heilongjiang and Ussuri Rivers were in the sphere of the Chinese territories; the Treaty of Nerchinsk from the legal point of view fixed the Eastern sector of the Sino-Russian border; in the second part of the 19th century Tsarist Russia forced the Qing government to sign a series of treaties - all these treaties were unequal for China.

"A series of books which appeared after 1976 signify a new level in studying the history of Sino-Russian relations... This level of studying is characterized by works not only on territorial questions between Russia and China: In time the Chinese historians began an all-out studying of all stages of Russian aggression toward China.

"To help the fruitful developing of research on the theme in the North, North-West, and North-East of China, scholarly societies for studying the history of Sino-Russian relations were created as well as the periodical publication *The Problems of Sino-Russian relations*.[222]

The researcher Huang Gu has come practically to the same conclusions, summarizing 40 years' worth of studying the history of Sino-Russian relations in the People's Republic of China in another survey article.[223]

The publishing house *Renmin Chubanshe* in April 1990 has published two books of the 4th volume of *The History of the Aggression of Tsarist Rus-*

---

[222] Lu Shuyong. "A Brief Description of Studies on Chinese Ties with Foreign Countries after the Creation of the People's Republic of China". *Shixue Jikan*. #3. 1989. P.50.

[223] Huang Gu. "General Description of Chinese Ties with Foreign Countries After the Creation of the People's Republic of China". *Zhongguoshi Yanjiu Dongtai*. #6. 1989.

sia in China, the major current "open" publication in the field that appeared in the last years in China.[224] This volume was prepared in the end of 1987 at the Institute of Modern history of the Chinese Academy of Social Sciences by a group of renown Chinese historians: Lü Yiran, Lü Cunkuan, Yang Shihao, Li Jiagu, Yu Shenwu, Zhang Zhiyi, Xu Yuebiao, Xue Xiantian, Kang Youming. The chief editor of the volume is Yu Shengwu, the editors are Lü Cunkuan and Xu Yuebiao.

The 4th volume of *The History of the Aggression of Tsarist Russia in China* summarizes the fundamental research of the theme by the Chinese historians and simultaneously adds a new dimension to the Chinese concept of the history of Sino-Russian relations and the history of formation of the Sino-Russian border, marking a shift in some Chinese conceptions. In some way the appearance of the volume symbolizes the new stage of the Chinese research: a wide scope of different materials allows to impregnate the concept with the historical texture, making it much more convincing and seductive to the reader.[225]

This volume differs from previous not only by the concept, which is quite more "scholarly", but also by the source base. The authors have used about 160 Chinese primary sources (a considerable part of these sources consists of a large amount of volumes (each consisting of several *juan*), and it is the first time that the overwhelming majority of these volumes are used in such an extent in academic research), 126 publications in Russian (various collections of documents, published in Russia and the Soviet Union, for example, the well-known publication "The Red Archives," the works by the scholars of the pre-revolutionary period as A.A. Batorskyi, V.V. Golitsin, A.N. Kuropatkin etc., Soviet historians of the early Soviet period as M.N.Pokrovskyi, I.M. Maiskyi, B.A. Romanov and the Soviet authors of 1950s and 1960s as M.S. Kapitsa, L.N. Kutakov, A.L. Narochnitskyi etc. (Soviet researches of the 1970s and 1980s are not used in the book), 156 publications in Western languages (Archives of the Foreign Office, the so-called "Blue books" of the British Parliament, different agreements on Tibet, Manchuria etc., published German diplomatic documents of 1871-1914, memoirs of Western state figures and diplomats of different countries (Churchill etc.) and state figures from Tsarist Russia such as A. Lobanov-Rostovskyi, D. Abrikosov, A. Izvolskyi, and Western researchers on the Russo-Chinese relations, but only of those whose

---

[224] *Sha E Qin Hua Shi.* (History of the Aggression of Tsarist Russia in China). Vol. 4. Beijing. 1990.
[225] Wen Xin. "Reviewing the 4th Volume of *History of the Aggression of Tsarist Russia in China. Jindaishi Yanjiu.* #6. 1988. P. 313.

scholarly positions are close to the scholarly positions of the Chinese researchers), and about 40 works of Japanese scholars.

Chronologically the volume involves the period of 1895-1917. In the foreword to the volume the Chinese authors stress that the book "described the aggressive operations of the Tsarist Russia toward China during the period of Imperialism, the aggression of Russian bourgeois Provisional Government toward China and raids of the whites on Chinese territories after the October revolution."[226]

In the author's opinion, the territorial division of the world was already complete at the time of the October Revolution, and the struggle for the imperialist redivision of the world has begun. Consequently, Russia took part in this redivision. The Chinese researchers emphasize that Russia sought to achieve the following strategic goals: "To take possession of those Chinese territories within the vicinity of the Great Wall," to extend its influence south of the Wall, "to weaken and to conquer the competitor" (i.e., China) and to assume "the leading role in Eastern Asia." The authors also stress the fact that while the international environment was in a state of constant flux, and "Russia constantly altered its strategic plans toward China; but up to the end of the Romanov's dynasty, Russia did not waver from the afore-mentioned strategic goals of its policy."[227]

In the foreword to the book the authors also present a detailed concept of "the history of Tsarist Russian aggression in China," which becomes the conceptual pivot of the book. In accord with this concept, the authors analyze and then present, in a very precise manner, the following stages:

1. *1895-1905.* The stage centered on the Russo-Japanese War, and the crisis of statehood in China, "when Russia, taking advantage of the situation, had began its policy of large-scale aggression," with the intention of "seizing" southeastern China, Xinjiang, Mongolia, Tibet and neighboring Korea.[228]

This stage is divided, by the author, into *two periods* before and after 1900; i.e., before and after "the armed seizure of the three northeastern Chinese provinces by Russia."[229]

During the *initial period* (1895-1900), Russia "gradually moved to subdue" the Qing government, and using economic means, "peacefully"

---

[226] *Sha E Qin Hua Shi.* P.1.
[227] *Ibid.* See also Chaprer 1, Section 1.
[228] *Ibid.* P. 3.
[229] *Ibid.*

seized the northeastern China.[230] The primary landmarks of this period were: the signing of the Sino-Russian Treaty of 1896; the granting of a loan by the French banks with the mediation of Russia (the loan has been viewed as unfavorable to China by Chinese scholars); and the building of the Chinese-Eastern Railway, which "meant the encompassing of northeastern China with the Russia sphere of influence."[231] The authors stress that Russian policy was a policy of "military Imperialism," and that Russia was competing with Germany and Japan in a struggle for spheres of influence. According to the authors Russia was the "initiator" of creating the crisis to "divide Chinese territory.[232]" Authors also attempt to illustrate how Russia and Great Britain "divided Pamir," and concluded an agreement concerning the building of railways[233] and the division of Chinese territories to the "north of the Great Chinese Wall," and in the Yangtze River basin.[234]

In 1900 "Russia, with Great Britain, Japan, Germany, France and the USA" took part in the suppression of the Boxer (*Yihetuan*) Uprising. The authors emphasized that while Russia proclaimed itself "a friend of China," declared that it would not seize even a smallest part of Chinese territory and would unilaterally withdrew its troops from Peking, Russian government received the largest indemnity from China compared with the other Western states[235].

During the author's *second period* (1900-1905), Russia attempted to legalize the military seizure of northeastern China for keeping it thereafter in its possession. The seizure of northeastern China by Russia, as the Chinese researchers show, aggravated Russia's relationship with Japan, Great Britain and the USA. Military conflicts between Russia and Japan in northeastern China led to a considerable loss of Chinese population[236].

2. 1906-1917. The distinguishing feature of the author's second stage (1906-1917) of "Russian aggression against China" was "the establishing of its union with Japanese militarism." And while Russia did lose southern Manchuria, it nevertheless continued "expansionist activity in northern

---

[230] See Chapter 1, Section 2.
[231] *Ibid.* P.3; See also Chapter 1, Section 3.
[232] *Ibid.* P.3.
[233] *Ibid.* P. 3. See also Chapter 1, Section 5.
[234] *Ibid.* P.3.
[235] *Ibid.* P. 4; See also Chapter 2.
[236] See Chapter 3.

and western China." "It was during this stage that practically one third of the Chinese territory fell into the Russian sphere of influence."[237]

This stage is divided by the Chinese researchers into the following periods:

A. 1906-1910, when the defeat of Russia in the Russo-Japanese War entirely remolded the balance of power in Asia. It was at this time that not only did Japan become the dominant military force in Asia, but the USA's military power increased to the point where it became a serious threat to Russian and Japanese interests. Tense relationships between both Russia and Germany and between Great Britain and Germany were sharpening and forming the base for the anti-German union between Great Britain and Russia. It was within this political environment that the tsarist government attempted "to coordinate its aggressive course against China" with the policies of the Great Britain and Japan.[238] During 1907 the Franco-Japanese and the Russo-English agreements were signed, as well as the secret agreement between Russian and Chinese imperial governments aimed against the Chinese people.[239] It was this process, according to the authors, that "strengthened the position of Russia in the Far East, and provided favorable conditions for a new wave of aggression from Tsarist Russia against China."[240]

It was during this period that the aim of Russia's aggressive actions was "to strengthen its colonial activity and monopolist position in northern Manchuria, and its expansionist aspirations in Outer Mongolia."[241] Tsarist Russia aspired to reach agreement with Japan concerning the mutual recognition of the division of "the spheres of influence" in a way that Korea should be considered in the Japanese "sphere of influence," and Outer Mongolia in Russian. Simultaneously Russia "recognized the preference" of Great Britain in Tibet in exchange for the recognition of Russian "special interests" in the Outer Mongolia and Central Asia.[242]

---

[237] *Ibid.* P.3.
[238] *Ibid.* P.5.
[239] *Ibid.*
[240] *Ibid.*
[241] *Ibid.* P.5-6.
[242] *Ibid.* P.6; See also Chapter 3.

B. **1911-1914.** The period, when Russia was ready "to begin a large-scale military action against Japan in the Chinese territories."[243] During this time the most known Russian actions "for the division of Chinese territory" were its efforts to give "independence" (inverted commas used by the Chinese researchers) for Outer Mongolia and Barga, and the well-known steps of Great Britain to give "independence" to Tibet.[244] In 1914 Russia "secretly seized the Chinese territory of Tannu-Uryanhai (now the Tuva Republic of the Russian Federation) with a territory of 170 thousand sq. km,[245] and using the commercial agreement in Manzhouli (Manchuria) seized 1400 sq. km of Chinese territory from the Greater Khingan mountain range to the West of Barga, invaded Ili, Kashgar, and Altai, willing "to transform Xinjiang into the territory totally dependent on Russia,"[246] strengthened its political control in Northern Manchuria, seeking that the territories with the railways in the eastern provinces of China be part of "Russian administrative system" and to substantiate traditional Russian plans of creating *Zheltorossia* (The Asian Russia).[247] In this period Russia signed the third secret agreement with Japan, widening the sphere of its influence to the Western part of the Outer Mongolia.[248]

C. **1915-1917.** The period, when after the beginning of the World War I the main interests of Russia, England, France and Germany were concentrated in Europe, but at a time also, as the authors of the book think, Russia "indulged Japan and victimized China."[249] Exercising this policy, Russia in 1915 managed to achieve "a weakening of the Chinese sovereign rights in the Outer Mongolia," and then the "autonomy" of Barga, "transforming these territories into Russian colony."[250] In 1916 Russia and Japan signed a fourth secret agreement, and that fact means "the official creation of a predatory coalition and the widening of the sphere of influence for Japan and Russia from the territories of Outer Mongolia up to the whole of China and the whole of the Far East."[251] In March 1917 Tsarist Russia, "victimizing China," achieved "a secret mutual understanding"

---

[243] Ibid; See Chapter 6.
[244] Ibid. Chapter 3, Sections 4,5,6,7.
[245] Ibid. P.6; See Chapter 5, Section 9.
[246] Chapters 5,7,8.
[247] Chapter 5, Section 1.
[248] Ibid. P.6; Chapter 5, Section 10.
[249] Ibid. P.7.
[250] Ibid.
[251] Ibid. P.7; Chapter 5, Section 10.

with Japan and supported the Japanese claims for "hereditary rights" on German possessions in Shandong province.[252]

It is almost certain that the book also follows in general the early Chinese concept for the history of Sino-Russian relations and the history of the formation of the Sino-Russian border, but the Chinese analysis here represents in a way a shift toward the new political situation: "The history of Russian aggression toward China" was shown by Chinese scholars only up to 1917 (i.e., up to the October revolution in Russia), and after the October revolution the word "aggression" was mentioned only in the case of tsarist diplomats, who did not recognize the government of Soviet Russia (the Russian envoy Kudashev, Annenkov etc.), the supporters of Kolchak, Semenov, Bakich, Horvat, and several organizations of the white Russians.

The authors emphasized that:

> "The Great October socialist revolution in Russia overthrew the Tsarist autocracy and the reactionary domination of the bourgeois Provisional government, and has opened a new era in the history of the humankind. The first socialist state in the world -- Soviet Russia, has openly declared a complete rupture with the traditional aggressive course of the Tsarist government toward China, and established a relationship between the two states on the basis of complete equality."[253]

The last pages of the book tell the "glorious stories" how Soviet and Chinese troops defeated the remnants of the white detachments in the regions of Central Asia (Ili, Xinjiang) and thus "made an end to the long-lasted aggression of Russia toward China."[254] After the collapse of the Soviet Union, Chinese scholars simply ceased to publish articles concerning Russia in the "open" scholarly journals, seeing Russia as a source of instability and ideological perturbation for China. But the problem of how to assess the Sino-Russian history still exists because Russia is now turning to its historical roots. The historical legacy of the Russian Federation in many cases is based now on disproving the Soviet period and reinventing the history of Tsarist Russia.

---

[252] Chapter 5, Section 10.
[253] Ibid. P. 970.
[254] Ibid. P. 1009.

3. CHINESE APPRAISALS OF RUSSIAN CONCEPTS

In 1990 the Chinese researcher Li Jiagu published an article "The Evolution of the Points of View of Soviet Historians on Sino-Russian Relations.[255]" In this article the author tries to analyze Soviet research on the theme, to emphasize the divergences in the points of view of Soviet historians, and the evolution of their ideas during the whole history of the Soviet state. This article, as the author stressed in the short foreword, was written for the benefit of "developing contacts between Russian and Chinese historians.[256]"

In his article Li Jiagu characterizes four stages of Soviet historical studies and analyzes the differences in the points of views of Soviet scholars. On the first stage (November 1917 - mid-1930s), according to Li Jiagu, the Soviet scholars:

> "condemned the plundering course of Russia towards China, criticized the scholars of Tsarist Russia, who misrepresented the history of the Sino-Russian relations; these [Soviet] scholars thought, that in the early stage of the Sino-Russian relationship the tsarist colonizers had seized Chinese territory, and that the Sino-Russian Treaty of Nerchinsk, signed in 1869, was unequal.[257]"

To confirm his conclusions he cited the works of S. Bakhrushin, who as Li Jiagu shows, wrote, that "the basin of the Heilongjiang (Amur) River was Chinese territory,[258]" as well as the books and articles of other prominent scholars as V. Avarin, B. Romanov, M. Pokrovskyi, V. Savin, K. Kharnskyi etc. Li Jiagu writes, that "at the time the Soviet scholars thought that the Treaty of Aigun (1858), the Sino-Russian Treaty of Tientsin, and the Treaty of Peking (1860) have unequal character; they condemned the predatory policy of Tsarist Russia toward China.[259]" According to his opinion, Soviet scholars were writing at the time that Tsarist Russia "seized the lands along the shores of Amur and Ussuri,[260]" forced China to sign the "unequal Treaty of Ili," and "cut the lands of Tannu-Uryanhai.[261]"

---

[255] *Jindaishi Yanjiu.* #3. 1990.
[256] *Ibid.* P. 245.
[257] *Ibid.* P.246.
[258] *Ibid.*
[259] *Ibid.*
[260] *Ibid.* P. 246-247.
[261] *Ibid.*

In a series of articles published in the journal *Red Archives* Soviet historians, according to Li Jiagu, "exposed the economic and cultural aggression of Tsarist Russia toward China.[262]" This section of the article ends with the following conclusion:

> "The point of view of Russian historians on the question of Sino-Russian relations was correct only up until the mid-1930s. After the October revolution the Soviet Union came out against aggression, supported the revolutionary struggle of all peoples, and kept the course of proletarian internationalism toward China, because the Soviet state was under the military interference of imperialist powers or under the threat of this interference. This situation was reflected in works on the course of Sino-Russian history, where the aggressive course of Tsarist Russia toward China was condemned and its criminal activities were exposed."[263]

On the second stage, that according to the author's concept lasted from the end of 1930s up to 1956, i.e., until the 20th Congress of the Communist Party of the Soviet Union, the Soviet historians, "being influenced by Stalinist chauvinism," "misrepresented" the history of Sino-Russian relations.[264] At the time, as Li Jiagu writes, Soviet scholars criticized the works of historians of the early Soviet period, especially the ideas of the school of Professor Pokrovskyi, that "was called an anti-Marxist, anti-Leninist, anti-scholarly" school.[265] The Chinese historian stresses:

> "It is obvious that many points of view of Stalin on the studying of historical problems were right. But with the strengthening of his power, his great-Russian nationalism and chauvinism was rising, and that was the reason for his changing several of his correct notions on the external policy of Russia."[266]

In this connection Li Jiagu thoroughly analyzes the ideas of Engels, Lenin, Armand and Stalin on different questions of the external policy of Tsarist Russia and makes the conclusion, that "under the influence of Stalin's chauvinism, the Soviet historians in late 1930s began to misrepresent the history of Sino-Russian relations and to embellish the aggressive course of

---

[262] *Ibid.*
[263] *Ibid.* P. 248.
[264] *Ibid.*
[265] *Ibid.*
[266] *Ibid.* P.249.

Russia toward China.²⁶⁷" For example, in the works by Russian historians A. Guber and L. Duman the history of the Treaty of Nerchinsk was described differently from the version of the early Soviet period, these historians, as shown by Li, stressed "the unequal character" of this treaty for Russia, showed that according to this treaty "China had seized the territory of the Tsarist Russia," and because of this "the Treaty of Aigun and all other treaties that Russia forced China to sign up in the second part of the 19th century, and according to which the Chinese lands were seized, were called equal treaties, by which Russia returned the lands, that were lost earlier.²⁶⁸" Later, according to the Chinese author's point of view, all these ideas were enlarged in the works by G. Efimov, E. Zhukov, A. Kamanin, A. Narochnitskyi, M. Nechkina, I. Reisner. B. Rubtsov, M. Sladkovskyi and other well-known historians. In these works, as Li Jiagu writes, Russian explorer Nevelskoyi, who entered the Amur from the sea, was unreservedly hymned, "the aggression of Tsarist Russia in Outer Mongolia" was decorated and embellished,²⁶⁹ the "aggressive policy of Russian imperialism in China at the end of 19th - beginning of the 20th century" was called "friendly policy," and Russian "economic aggression" was shown as "equal commerce.²⁷⁰" This section of the article was ended by the following conclusion:

> "The point of view of Soviet scholars of this period was absolutely different from that of the early Soviet period. The historians of the early Soviet period impartially exposed the aggression of the Tsarist Russia toward China, but the Soviet historians of the second period embellished this aggression."²⁷¹

Then the Chinese historian analyzed the third stage which lasted from 1956 (i.e., from the 20th Congress of the Communist Party of the Soviet Union) till the 1960s (i.e., till the beginning of the Sino-Soviet border negotiations).²⁷² The main feature of this period was, as Li emphasizes, "the influence of the critique of Stalin's mistakes on the research of the history of Sino-Russian relations." During this period, "after criticizing the wrong points of views of Stalin," "Soviet historians condemned the wrong ten-

---

²⁶⁷ *Ibid.* P. 250.
²⁶⁸ *Ibid.* P. 250-251.
²⁶⁹ *Ibid.* P.252.
²⁷⁰ *Ibid.* P. 252.
²⁷¹ *Ibid.* P. 253-254.
²⁷² *Ibid.*

dency of embellishing the external policy of Tsarist Russia.²⁷³" For example, though in *Small Soviet Encyclopedia, Diplomatic Dictionary*, the schoolbook "World History," and in the books and articles by N. Shastina, P. Yakovleva and other Soviet scholars published at the time, it was stressed that "before the signing of the Treaty of Nerchinsk, the lands seized by tsarist colonizers were under nobody's ownership, and even declared that the Qing government had seized the lands of Tsarist Russia. Even scholars who developed these conceptions considered the Treaty of Nerchinsk as equal.²⁷⁴" According to the opinion of the Chinese scholar, during this period "an attempt was made to overcome the wrong tendency of embellishing tsarist policy toward China."²⁷⁵

The fourth period in Soviet social sciences relating to the history of Sino-Russian relations, according to Li's periodisation, began in the 1960s and is still going on. The Soviet historians, as Li thinks, pay attention now to the period up to the end of the 19th century, because most of the Sino-Russian treaties were signed during this time.²⁷⁶ These works have, according to Li Jiagu, an indecisive character, for example, A. Okladnikov, a renowned Russian scholar, on the one hand, wrote that "the colonizer activity of Tsarist Russia in the basin of the Amur River has a progressive character," emphasized that this region "never has been under Chinese jurisdiction," that "the ancestors of the native people who were living to the north of the Amur River and to the east of the Ussuri River even in the Neolith age have created an original culture" that had "no ties with Chinese tradition,²⁷⁷" but on the other hand recognized "the strong ties of the Chinese ancient culture with the cultural tradition of the native people of these regions" and showed "the progressive role" of these ties. A. Okladnikov also considered as "reliable" the information about the creation of an administration by the Ming dynasty (1368-1644) in these regions.²⁷⁸

The Chinese historians especially stress the central point of their modernized concept: on the one hand, it is "necessary to divide the truth and the lies in history, to define, that the treaties which established the Sino-Soviet border which were concluded in the second part of the 19th century - the beginning of the 20th century, when people of Russia and China were in a situation when they could not decide their own destiny; these

---

[273] *Ibid.* P. 254.
[274] *Ibid.*
[275] *Ibid.* P. 255-256.
[276] *Ibid.* P. 256.
[277] *Ibid.*
[278] *Ibid.*

treaties were forced by Russia,²⁷⁹" on the other hand "it is necessary on the basis of these unequal treaties to resolve completely the Sino-Soviet border question, and to define the border line on its entire extent.²⁸⁰" Li explains, that

> "China does not require the return of the Chinese territories seized by Tsarist Russia according to the Sino-Russian treaties. But the Soviet side does not declare the Sino-Russian border treaties, which were signed in the second part of the 19th century, unjust and unequal, and forced by the Tsarist Russia to China, and on the contrary considered the Willow Border and the Great Chinese Wall as the Chinese boundaries in the North. They think that the Chinese boundaries in the West should not exceed the borders of Gansu and Sichuan provinces."²⁸¹

After 1971, as Li Jiagu writes, a Soviet historians published many works, which "misrepresented the history of Chinese-Russian relations.²⁸²" The authors of these works, according to Li Jiagu were: V. Aleksandrov, E. Besprozvannikh, I. Zlatkin, V. Kabuzan, M. Kapitsa, G. Melikhov, V. Miasnikov, A. Narochnitskyi, S. Tikhvinskyi and others Soviet scholars.²⁸³ In these works they write how the character of Russian foreign policy toward China differs from that of the Western powers which pursued aggressive policy. They stress that Russia returned the lands that the Qing government has seized earlier in accordance with Sino-Russian treaties, and emphasize the fact that the Treaty of Nerchinsk was signed under Chinese military pressure.²⁸⁴

After 1985, as the Chinese author shows, the amount of works on Sino-Russian relations in Soviet historiography decreased considerably, but the point of views of Russian scholars remain unchanged. The second edition of the book by Corresponding Member of Russian Academy of Sciences V. Miasnikov *Russia and China in the 17th Century*, as Li Jiagu states, can only strengthen this idea.²⁸⁵

---

²⁷⁹ *Ibid.* P.257.

²⁸⁰ *Ibid.*

²⁸¹ *Ibid.*

²⁸² *Ibid.*

²⁸³ For the Russian bibliography on Sino-Russian relations consult my forthcoming book *The Sino-Russian St.Petersburg Treaty of 1881: Diplomatic History.*

²⁸⁴ *Ibid.* P. 258.

²⁸⁵ *Ibid.* P.260. This simplistic view only proves that Russian literature of the late 1980s on border problems was not available for the author's analysis.

In the conclusion to his article Li stresses, that "the ideas of Soviet scholars shortly after the October revolution, i.e., on the early stages, were more or less close to the truth," but then "the Soviet scholars misrepresented the history of Sino-Russian relations and began to embellish the policy of Tsarist Russia toward China.[286]" Li Jiagu writes, that "Sino-Russian relations were developing under circumstances that Russian and Chinese people could [not] decide their own destiny, which is why the Soviet and Russian people are not responsible" for these treaties.[287] At the present time, according to the author, Sino-Soviet relations are "moving toward a destination of normalization." The normalization which was formally declared in 1989 was unanimously approved by the people of the two states, and this is the reason why the two countries can see in the future positive results in the history of Sino-Soviet relations.[288]

---

[286] *Ibid.*
[287] *Ibid.*
[288] *Ibid.*

RUSSIAN APPROACHES

A. RUSSIAN CONCEPTS AND THE PROBLEM OF 'BALANCED' INTERPRETATION OF THE RUSSIAN-CHINESE RELATIONS

1. RUSSIAN APPROACHES

Notable contributions which have aided in the detailing of Soviet and Russian ideas concerning the history of international relations in Asia have recently been rendered by Soviet and Russian historians from various generations, such as: V.A. Aleksandrov, Ye.L. Besprozvannykh, A.A. Bokshchanin, L.A. Borovkova, A.I. Chernyshov, N.F. Demidova, D.V. Dubrovskaya, S.N.Goncharenko, Ye.A. Grigoryeva, B.P. Gurevitch, A.S. Ipatova, D.A. Isiyev, M.S. Kapitsa, G.S. Karetina, K.Sh. Khafizova, A. Khodzhayev, A.N. Khokhlov, V.S. Kuznetsov, N.S. Kuleshov, A.G. Malyavkin, G.V. Melikhov, I.T. Moroz, V.S. Miasnikov, V.A. Moiseyev, A.L. Narochnitskyi, N.Yu. Novgorodskaya, G.N. Romanova, N.V. Shepeleva, Ye.D. Stepanov, A.I. Tarasova, S.L. Tikhvinskyi, I.S. Yermachenko, L.V. Zabrovskaya, O.V. Zotov, and others.[289] But the new Russian approaches are very fragile because the whole state is in a process of searching for national identity, and because of this these new concepts are vulnerable to the current political struggles in Russia.

---

[289] See: *Nauchniye Trudi Sotrudnikov Instituta Dalnego Vostoka Rossiiskoi Akademii Nauk (1968-1991). Bibliograficheskyi Ukazatel.* (The Academic Works of the Institute of Far Eastern Studies. Russian Academy of Sciences. (1968-1991). Bibliography Index). Moscow, 1992; *Biobibliograficheskyi Slovar Rossiiskikh Vostokovedov.* (Biobibliographical Dictionary of Russian Orientalists). Moscow. 1994, and also the bibliography on Sino-Russian relations in my forthcoming book *The Sino-Russian St.Petersburg Treaty of 1881: Diplomatic History* .

In the previous chapter -- which was concerned with Chinese approaches toward Sino-Russian history -- those key points where divergences between Russian and Chinese concepts are evident, were shown. Chinese scholars attributed various trends in Soviet and Russian historiography to separate periods of Soviet history.[290] It is more likely, however, that there have always been only two trends in the Russian and Soviet representations of the history of Sino-Russian relations. The first of these two trends fully approves the Russian policy of expansion, i.e., seeking geographical boundaries which would allow for the stable functioning of the Russian Empire and for the defence of its borders.[291] This trend, which depicts Tsarist Russia's colonization policies within the new territories as positive steps, has always flourished the most when the Russian/Soviet state's power is at its peak.

The second of these two trends, which has tended to be more balanced, not only sees Russia as a link between different civilizations and thus as a mediator between China and the West, but also shows the negative as well as the positive implications of the Russian policies toward "smaller" nationalities and China and stresses only within certain historical periods the objective necessity of seeking defendable natural boundaries for the Russian state with a minimum of military force involved to maintain peaceful coexistence with the outside world.[292] It should be noted in this respect that it was the emphasis on Russia's *national* interests that was made by certain researchers, and the emphasis on Russia's *state* (imperial) interests that was made by other researchers which resulted in the disparate interpretations of Sino-Russian relations among the historians working during the Soviet period. Naturally this emphasis was usually predetermined by not only "personal affinities" but also by political considerations.

Practically all researchers (excluding those of the new generation which emerged in the 1980s) have embraced both approaches though one or the other usually prevails in any published text.[293] Even those Russian

---

[290] Li Jiagu. "Evolution of the Point of View of Soviet Historians on the History of Russian-Chinese Relations". *Jindaishi Yanjiu*. #3, 1990.

[291] V.S. Miasnikov, N.V. Shepeleva. *Imperiya Tsin i Rossya v XYII- Nachale XX V.* (The Qing Empire and the Russian State in the 17th - Early 20th Centuries), in: *Kitai i Sosedi v Novoye i Noveishee Vremya* (China and its Neighbors in Modern and Contemporary Times) Ed. by S.L. Tikhvinskyi. Moscow. 1982; V.S. Miasnikov. *The Ch'ing Empire and the Russian State in the 17th Century*. English translation of the revised Russian text. Moscow. 1985.

[292] See, for example, *The Academic Conference "State and Society of China"*. Abstracts. Moscow. 1970-1995.

[293] Best examples of these can be found in the book *Chapters from the History of Russo-Chinese Relations, 17th-19th Centuries*. Moscow. 1985.

researchers who analyzed early Russian-Chinese contacts from the point of view of the contact's "imparity" for Russia and stressed the aggressive character of the Qing Empire's foreign policy, have now found it more fruitful to shift to the more sophisticated (yet during the Soviet period, more unacceptable) "modernizational approach." This approach consists of analyzing Sino-Russian relations within a framework of different cultural and religious traditions of dealing with diplomatic counter-agents within a general framework of moving ("modernizing") from the Feudalism toward Capitalism. These researchers no longer insist on emphasizing the aggressive character of early Qing policy toward its neighbors as before, but instead concentrate on the impossibility of a correlation between Asian (Chinese, Confucian) and Western (Russian, Christian) tradition in establishing balanced and equal diplomatic relations. For example, Professor V. Miasnikov, who -- with a large amount of original Chinese and Russian archival documents -- had once substantiated the concept of the "aggressive policies of the Kangxi emperor" against Russia and Mongolia, emphasizes that:

> "Research [of the] Russian-Chinese relations within the framework of international relations raises a problem of typology of the interconnection between Russia and China. As provided by historical evidence, the contacts of states of the same, for example, European civilizations are remarkably dissimilar to the contacts of the states that developed within different civilizations. The traditions of culture that in many ways predetermine the political culture of any society, have their impact upon all levels of the foreign political process... [The] Political culture of Russia was based on the norms of Christian morality and European tradition, that implied equality of all sovereign states; Meanwhile, China's political culture was based on the Confucian principles of political hierarchy and the Sinocentrist perception of the surrounding world. European and Russian political traditions were mainly aimed at building horizontal ties among various states. In the 17th - 19th centuries Russia and China were two feudal powers quite comparable in terms of their political, economic and cultural dimensions. Thus the Russian side tended to see their political communication as [a] contact between equal actors in international relations, i.e., along a horizontal line. Chinese political culture actually excluded equality from China's relations with any country of the world. China was willing to build all its international ties along a vertical line."[294]

---

[294] Vladimir S. Miasnikov. Ethno-Cultural Aspects of the Interaction between Russia and China and Their Influence upon Soviet-Chinese Relations, in: *Sino-Soviet Affairs*, Vol. XV, #4. Winter 1991/2. P. 88. Cited exactly as the text was printed in English.

Interestingly enough, the break up of the Soviet Union dealt such a heavy blow to the former Soviet social sciences that those researchers who survived the collapse of the Soviet mainstream paradigms managed to come closer to a more balanced understanding of the historical processes in their related fields. This has provided for the incorporation of Chinese concepts and for the elaboration of a more balanced approach to the Chinese' highly ideological theme.

2. CREATING A BALANCED CONCEPT: RUSSIAN-CHINESE TREATY ACTS — POSSIBLE APPROACHES AND INTERPRETATIONS

This section attempts to review the recent conclusions made by Russian social sciences concerning the above-cited agenda in order to discover a way to a more balanced interpretation of Russian-Chinese relations.[295] This conceptual framework is not an "end result" in itself, but an attempt to create a common base for further discussion in the field.

The peoples of Russia and China first discovered the existence of one another in the 13th century, when the Mongolians, in their attempts to conquer Russia, brought Russian prisoners of war to Peking, which at that time was ruled by the Mongolian dynasty of Yuan (1271-1368). The Russian captives eventually came to represent a special unit in the Emperor's guards.[296]

The exploration of Siberia (through military means, as well as others) -- which began with the Russian pioneer-Cossacks in the late 16th century -- caused the building of many new towns in the region. The 1650s saw the

---

[295] This section is based on transformed Russian concepts which emerged in the 1980s. These concepts for their part were influenced by the earlier ideas elaborated by V.A. Aleksandrov, A.L. Narochnitskyi, P.Ye. Skachkov, S.L. Tikhvinskyi. The later concept was formulated and developed in: V.S. Miasnikov. N.V. Shepeleva. "The Qing Empire and Russia in the 17th - Early 20th Centuries". *Kitai i Sosedi v Novoye i Noveisheye Vremya* (China and its Neighbors in Modern and Contemporary Times). Moscow. 1982; V.S. Miasnikov. *Imperiya Tsin i Russkoye Gosudarstvo v XVII*. (The Qing Empire and the Russian State in the 17th Century) 2nd revised and supplemented edition. Khabarovsk. 1987; V.S. Miasnikov. *The Ch'ing Empire and the Russian State in the 17th Century*. English translation of the revised Russian text. Moscow. 1985; V.S. Miasnikov. A.D. Voskressenski. "On the History of Sino-Russian and Sino-Soviet Relations". *Vestnik MID SSSR* (The Newsletter of the Foreign Ministry of the USSR). #22. 1988; O.A. Glushkova. "The Position of the Russian Government toward China in the '6Os of the 18th Century". *15th Academic Conference "State and Society of China"*. Vol. 2. Moscow. 1984; R.V. Makarova. "The Development of Sino-Russian Relations from the Mid-18th Century up to the 1860s". *Vneshnyaya Politika Rossii na Dalnem Vostoke* (Russian Foreign Policy in the Far East). Moscow. 1983; A.N. Khokhlov. "Trade as the Priority Feature of Russian Policy Toward China, 1840s-1890s". *20th Academic Conference "State and Society in China"*. Vol. 2. Moscow. 1988.

[296] For detailed information see V.S. Miasnikov. "China's Knowledge about Russia in the 17th Century". *Voprosy Istorii*. #2. 1985.

beginning of the economic exploration of those territories, i.e., the colonization of Siberia as an "economic territory." Edward L. Keenan is quite correct, stressing:

> "I would argue... that this was a state that expanded mightily, but was not "expansionist." That is, Muscovite and later Russian political actors were not motivated by a transcendent belief that they must expand or fail, that they were fated to expand, that they could ignore mundane pragmatic considerations and the risks and costs of expansion because they were unlike other mortals or their expansion was unlike other practical matters. Muscovites typically behaved as pragmatic opportunists, relatively risk-averse, and quite willing to give up any objective when resisted or when the goals become too costly. These were not Crusaders..."[297]

This view is equally supported by Alfred J. Rieber:

> "The myth of unlimited Russian expansionism deserves a final interment. There is no foundation for a belief in Russian messianism. There was no imperial plan either for expanding or administering the empire. The struggle over the borderlands was... a multi-state competition among the flank powers over the legacy of the declining steppe empires."[298]

By the early 19th century capitalism took roots in Russia -- though not in the same way as it did in the West. Capitalism in Russia was initiated mainly "from above," and reached its peak at the same time as the West was entering its age of Imperialism. In Russia, it was only by the end of the 19th century that capitalism acquired imperialistic features, yet it still retained forms of feudalism and semi-feudalism.

The immense Russian Empire (much like the Chinese Empire) did have its own colonial domains -- the peripheral territories. However, the issue of the peripheral territories needs to be taken under special consideration, since those peripheral lands cannot be considered as "classic" colonies. These territories were incorporated within Russia's borders, and

---

[297] Edward L. Keenan. "On Certain Mythical Beliefs and Russian Behaviors". P. 21-22. Paper delivered in May 3, 1993 at the workshop "Influence of History on the Foreign Policy of Russia" in the framework of the Russian Littoral Project, sponsored by The Paul H. Nitze School of Advanced International Studies, The Johns Hopkins University and Department of Government and Politics, University of Maryland at College Park.

[298] Alfred J. Rieber. "Struggle Over the Borderlands". P.42. Paper delivered in May 3, 1993 at the workshop "Influence of History on the Foreign Policy of Russia" in the framework of the Russian Littoral Project, sponsored by The Paul H. Nitze School of Advanced international Studies, Johns Hopkins University and Department of Government and Politics, University of Maryland at College Park.

their acquisition, lasting for many decades, involved far more complex processes than that of a simple colonial conquest. Yet, at the same time, the peripheral lands of the Russian Empire did represent both of the historically known types of colonial domains: those populated by re-settlers (Siberia, Northern Kazakhstan) and those by subjugated natives (Central Asia).

As a result of backward agrarian relations in the center, the least intensive colonization of these scarcely populated lands in Siberia was not immediately followed by rapid economic development; however, it provided an impulse for the cultural and economic development of the territory. While the measures taken then by the Russian government and the local administrations met the interests of those in power at the center, they also contributed to the development of productive forces in those remote territories, i.e., they were beneficial to the periphery.[299]

With the unification of the old Ming dynasty's territories (1438-1644) with Manchuria as such under the new Manchu rulers, as well as the following annexation of several Mongolian principalities which resulted from many highly destructive wars, the northern borders of the Qing Empire (1644-1911) stretched beyond the Great Chinese Wall, which had been considered as the traditional socio-cultural boundary of the Chinese Empire in the north—though, throughout various periods of history, the Chinese civilization's sphere of influence (in whatever form) had stretched far beyond that line.[300] It was after this unification that the laws which provide for the stable functioning of the Empire went to work, thus creating a situation which required the Qing Empire to establish contacts with the Russian state[301] and thus to ensure its borders.

Gradually, relations between the two states were continually taken into consideration, and by the end of the 17th century both Russia and

---

[299] For detailed information consult, for example, V.A. Aleksandrov. *Rossiya na Dalnevostochnikh Rubezhakh [Vtoraya Polovina 17 Veka].* (Russia in its Far Eastern Boundaries [Second half of the 17th Century]). 2nd supplemented edition. Khabarovsk. 1984; A.I. Alekseev, G.V. Melikhov. "The Discovery and First Attempts of Russians to Colonize Near-Amuria and the Maritime Territories". *Voprosy Istorii.* #3. 1984; I.S. Ribachenok. "Russian Far Eastern Policy of the 1900s on the Pages of the Russian Conservative Press". *Vneshnyaya Politika Rossii i Obschestvennoye Mneniye* (Russian Foreign Policy and Public Opinion). Moscow. 1988.

[300] Nevertheless some Russian researchers believe that the so-called "Willow Border" was the northern border of the Manchu Empire. G.V. Melikhov. "Willow Border - the Border of the Qing Empire". *Voprosy Istorii.* #8. 1981.

[301] Ye.N. Ryabinin, O.V. Shatalov. "The First Russo-Chinese Treaties as a Reflection of the Geographical Knowledge about the South of the Far East in Late 17th - Early 18th Centuries". *Problemy Krayevedeniya* (The Problems of Local History). Ussuryisk. 1989.

China felt the need for such relations to be institutionalized.[302] In 1689 the two states signed the Treaty of Nerchinsk -- the first treaty between Qing China and a foreign state, which, to a certain extent, predetermined the very character of Sino-Russian relations up to the mid-19th century. Apart from the issues of territorial demarcation, the treaty also contained trade related provisions.

When Boyar Golovin arrived at the Nerchinsk negotiations from Moscow, he was accompanied by fifteen hundred troops; the Qing ambassadors appeared at Nerchinsk with twelve thousand troops. Russian historians generally agree that Golovin, due to the pressure imposed upon him from the other side and to his own lack of information (in fact, the Qing emperor *needed* peace with the Russians to reassert his forces against the Dzungar Khanate), was impelled to give up Albazin and to give up the Russian-explored lands on the right side of the Argun River and across the upper and middle stream of the Amur as far as the Bureya River which made up a larger part of the Albazin territory.[303] The territories south of the Uda River (i.e., almost all of Lower Amuria) were left undemarcated. Simultaneously the Manchu ambassador vowed the Qing Empire's commitment not to populate the Albazin lands.[304]

The Treaty of Nerchinsk did not determine the Sino-Russian border in the usual sense of the term. From the upper Argun River, the border went on to the juncture with the Shilka River, with the north bank remaining within Russian domains, and the south bank being allocated to Qing China. From the upper Argun River, the border was demarcated along the Gorbitsa River up to its source. Because at the time the mountain ranges in Amuria had not yet been thoroughly explored, the Russian text of the Treaty read that the borderline would continue eastward from the source of the Gorbitsa River along the "Kamenny (Rocky) Mountains... [and] stretch onward to the sea," while the Manchu text named those mountains differently as the Amba Khingan.[305] As seen by the Russian experts, the Treaty of Nerchinsk, as far as the legal side was and is concerned, does not correspond to either contemporary or past norms of international law.

---

[302] See, for example, V.S.Miasnikov. "China's Knowledge about Russia in the 17th Century"; V.S. Miasnikov. "New Knowledge about Russia in China of the 17th Century". *Vsemirnaya Istoriya i Vostok* (World History and the Orient). Moscow. 1989; N.Yu. Novgorodskaya. "Russia in the Works by Yu Zhengxie (1775-1840)". *16th Academic Conference "State and Society in China"*. Vol. 2. Moscow. 1985.

[303] G.V. Melikhov. "How the Aggression of Qing China's Feudal Rulers Against Russian Settlers in Amuria in 1780s Was Prepared". *Dokumenty Oprovergayut* (Documents Refute). Moscow. 1982.

[304] V.S. Miasnikov. *The Ch'ing Empire and the Russian State in the 17th Century*. Moscow. 1985.

[305] *Russko-Kitaiiskiye Otnosheniya. 1689-1916. Ofitsialniye Documenty*. (Russian-Chinese Relations. 1689-1916. Official Documents). Moscow. 1958.

The geographical definitions in the text of the treaty are rather vague, schematic and too general; the two sides did not exchange any maps of the region nor any instruments of ratification; the two language texts are not identical, and the articles admit varying interpretation.

From the 18th century, the center of gravity in Sino-Russian relations had been shifting to Central Asia, where many regions were becoming the epicenter of not only Russian and Chinese activity, but of other states as well. Russia's movement toward southern Siberia and Kazakhstan was accompanied by the colonization of the territories and the development of agriculture and trade which reflected both the national and state interests of Russia.

This is the primary point of disagreement between Russian and Chinese scholars concerning the character of Sino-Russian relations. The Chinese scholars unanimously qualify the economic aspects of the Russian settlers' activities in the Far East and Central Asia as the "aggression of Russian Tsarism" and the "annexation of lands originally Chinese," while neither those lands nor their population had ever been fully incorporated within the traditional domains of the Chinese Empire. Therefore all Sino-Russian treaties -- except for the Treaty of Nerchinsk which had been signed under pressure imposed by the Qing Empire -- are being qualified by the Chinese historians as "unequal" and "forcefully imposed" upon China.

The 18th century saw the progressive development of Sino-Russian trade which gradually provided for the primary agendas of both Russia and China in their mutual relations. Evidently, that development was emphasized in 1857 by K. Marx (an authority in Communist China) when he wrote that:

> "Russia's relations with the Chinese Empire are altogether of a special kind... Since the Russians are excluded from maritime trade with China and have therefore never taken part or become involved in the former or contemporary squabbles over this matter, they escape the loathing that the Chinese have entertained since time immemorial for all foreigners who approached their coast... They are content to carry on an overland trade which is best suited for them.[306]"

In order to bring order to trade relations between the two countries, in 1726 the government of Catherine I send a mission led by S.L. Vladislavich-Raguzinskyi to Peking. During the new negotiations that

---

[306] K. Marx. "Russland Handel mit China", in: Marx/Engels. *Werke*. Vol. 12. Dietz Verlag. Berlin. 1973. P.153-154.

took place between 1726 and 1727, Russia and the Qing Empire adopted the principle that "each would possess what it possesses now" as a base for the border demarcation. In August 1727, the two sides signed the preliminary Treaty of Burinsk which determined the borderline from the mound of Abagaitu in the Argun River's upper basin (where the borderline coincided with the border by the Argun River as set by the Treaty of Nerchinsk, 1689) up to the Shabin-Dabaga Pass in the Greater Sayany Range. The Treaty of Burinsk was included as Article 3 in the Treaty of Kyakhta of 1727 which determined the political and trade relationship between Russia and the Qing Empire. The border, as established by those treaties, was demarcated by the special joint Russian-Manchurian commissions which provided descriptions of regions along with maps. Border-guard stations and beacons were built along the border, while Article 7 of the Treaty of Kyakhta confirmed the provisions of the Treaty of Nerchinsk about the lands that were left undemarcated.

After that, several missions were sent to Peking with the intention of expanding trade with China. With the regulation of trade relations becoming an ever more urgent issue, in 1861 the two sides entered negotiations that were crowned with the signing of the Treaty of Kulja.[307]

A noteworthy point to mention in this connection is that in classical Marxist terms, the character of foreign policy is determined by the social superstructure and economic basis. This idea prevailed in the former Soviet Union and is still the mainstream paradigm in Communist China. But the definition of policy as "the concentrated expression of the economy"[308] is disputable. Foreign policy also experiences influence from the current international situation, certain historical and cultural traditions, and many other factors. Correlation between the economy and policy can vary in every specific case under various circumstances following a complicated dependency on social, economic, and political factors. Besides, foreign policy is not at all a simple derivative from domestic policy, because when dealing outside the country, the ruling circles deal not with their own citizens but rather with the ruling circles of other countries.

Following up on these approaches, in the early 1990s Russian scholars started to elaborate upon concepts based on the difference between national interests (i.e., the needs of the society as a whole) and state interests (i.e., the needs which contribute to the consolidation of the external and

---

[307] N. Antonov. "On the History of Sino-Russian Kulja Treaty of 1851". *Dokumenty Oprovergayut* (Documents Refute). Moscow. 1982.

[308] V.I. Lenin. "Again, On the Trade Unions, the Current Moment and the Mistakes by Comrades Bukharin and Trotsky". *Polnoye Sobraniye Sochinenyi* (Complete Collected Works). Moscow. 1958-1965. Vol. 42. P. 278.

internal positions of the state [empire] to provide the most favorable conditions for its functioning).[309] While the development of national interests renders a prevailing influence on the formation of the state interests, state interests do not necessarily influence the overall formation of national interests. As it was noted by Russian researcher Ye.D. Stepanov, the author of the most scrupulous Russian analyses of the Chinese border policies of the 1980s as well as the founder of innovative theoretical approaches to Soviet and Russian foreign policies:

> "National interests can be at certain contradiction with state interests. For example, there can be a contradiction concerning such a seemingly undisputable issue as the safeguarding of national security. The requirement of the conditions for the peaceful and free development of society entirely corresponds to the vital tasks of foreign policy of any state and thus coincides with the state interests. However, while coinciding in the main point, the interests of the state and the society can be different in terms of the forms and methods of providing national security.[310]"

As for state interests (especially, regarding the historical past), they have been formed under the influence of class and group interests as well as the needs and ambitions of the elite which have always been marked by their subjective interpretation of reality, and which always tended to identify their own understanding as corresponding to the interests of the entire society.

The first lopsided treaties between the Western Powers and China were detrimental not only to Russia's foreign-policy, but to its trade and economic relations in eastern and Central Asia. As viewed by Russian historians, Russia's initially successful policy in Kazakhstan and its consolidation of its positions in Central Asia -- when the decrepiting Qing Empire was retreating under the assault of Western powers -- enabled Russia, through the signing of treaties with China, to open new possibilities in expanding trade contacts there.[311] This corresponded with the national

---

[309] The concept of the correlation between national and state interests was formulated by Ye.D. Stepanov in his article "The Notion of 'Interests' in Foreign Policy". *Problemy Dalnego Vostoka*. #3. 1990. In this connection I think that it is scholarly more correct to speak about the state interests and not about "intrinsic Russian aggressiveness" as an explanation of the activity of Russian pioneer-Cossacks and settlers in the Far East and Central Asia. For a detailed delineation of this concept and how it differentiates from basic Western concepts of nation-state and the role of the state (government) in the society see my introduction to the forthcoming book *Russia-China-U.S.A.: Redefining the Triangle* (Nova Science Publishers, Inc.).

[310] Ye. D. Stepanov. "The Notion of 'Interests' in Foreign Policy". P. 66.

[311] I do not discuss here questions relating to Sino-Russian trade because this is a special field. Primary Russian literature on the subject can be found in the bibliography to my forthcoming book *The Sino-Russian St. Petersburg Treaty of 1881: Diplomatic History* .

interests of both states, though in no way could be identified with their state (government) interests which were running counter to one another.

In the mid-19th century these lopsided treaties were in most cases based on the principle of the "most-favored-nation treatment". Apart from those provisions pertaining to the rights and benefits of foreigners within the sphere of trade and regulation, these agreements also contained provisions granting special rights to foreign powers and violated the sovereign rights and territorial integrity of China. The "most favored nation-principle," at the time, implied that individual benefits granted by China to any single counteragent would be extended to all other foreign states. Those provisions were first mentioned in the Sino-British Corollary Agreement of 1843, and then fixed for Russia in the Tientsin Treaty of 1858. These provisions were unequal for China, because it violated China's sovereignty.

Throughout the late 19th century, the interpower competition for the political and economic subjugation of China resulted in a unique form of lopsided treaty: those agreements which would determine the preferential rights of a foreign power within specified portions of Chinese territory. With these agreements, the Chinese government vowed not to transfer a particular part of its territory to any third power without the consent of the power signing the given agreement.[312] While in general these treaties pertained primarily to the economy, those provisions pertaining to the extraterritorial rights (including consular jurisdiction) for foreigners and those about the "lease" of Chinese territories all were direct violations of the territorial sovereignty of China.[313]

The mid-19th century witnessed radical changes in the international landscape of the East Asia. The Opium Wars, which resulted in the forceful opening of Chinese sea ports to British, French, and U.S. trade interests, marked the beginning of the Qing Empire's transformation into a semi-colonial country.[314] It was in this light that Russia sought to sign a treaty that would bring the Western powers' attempts to aggravate the

---

[312] For example, the British-Chinese agreement of 1894, the French-Chinese agreement of 1897, the British-Chinese agreement of 1898, and the Japanese-Chinese agreement of 1898.

[313] For example, the agreement between Germany and China on the "lease" of Jiaozhou in 1898, the agreement between France and China on the construction of the railways in South China in 1898, the Russian-Chinese agreement with France about the railways in the direction of the Russian border. See also Ye.A. Grigoryeva. Ye.D. Kostikov. "The Maoists' Speculation with the Notion "Unequal Treaty". *Problemy Dalnego Vostoka*. #1. 1975.

[314] The Russian position during the second Opium War was analyzed by S.I. Povalnikov. "The War of France and England Against China (the Second Opium War of 1856-1860) and the Positions of Russia". *Dokumenty Oprovergayut* (Documents Refute). Moscow. 1982.

Sino-Russian relationship to an end, and would cut off access to the Amur River to Western vessels. Such a treaty was signed at Aigun in 1858.

Article one of the Treaty of Aigun which figured out the border between the two stated:

> "Let the left bank of the Amur River, beginning from the Argun River and up to the maritime north of the Amur River, be the domain of the Russian state, while the right bank, downward along the stream to the Ussuri River be the domain of the Dai Qing state; let the lands and places, beginning from the Ussuri River and stretching on up the sea, before the border between the two states in those places is determined, be -- as it is now -- the common possession of the Dai Qing and the Russian state.[315]"

Through other articles within the Treaty of Aigun, the navigation in the Amur, Sungari and Ussuri Rivers was allowed only for vessels of the Russian and the Qing states. The Manchu population on the left bank of the Amur River was "to stay in the same places of their residence under the rule of the Manchu government...[316]" This did not necessarily mean, however, that Russia recognized China's sovereignty over the territory where these Manchu settlements were located. The text of the article said that the border was to be demarcated along the Amur River and that the mentioned territory was to be considered Russian, while the Qing government was merely granted jurisdiction over its citizens residing in that area of Russian territory.

As far as the general significance of the Aigun Treaty of 1858 is concerned, a Russian historiography shared the view that the treaty helped allow for the return of the left-side (to the north) of the Amur River's basin to Russia, which had been given up to China with the Treaty of Nerchinsk (1689). As for the lands on the right side (to the south) of the Amur and Argun Rivers, where some Russian settlements had been located before, they were not and could not be returned to Russia.

The Treaty of Aigun was very important in terms of settling relations between Russia and the Qing China; in particular, it eliminated the chances for border conflicts in the eastern periphery of Russia. The Treaty of Aigun also blocked British attempts to aggravate Qing China's relations with Russia and closed access to the Amur River for European vessels.

---

[315] *Russko-Kitaiiskiye Otnosheniya. 1689-1916. Ofitsialniye Documenty*. (Russian-Chinese Relations. 1689-1916. Official Documents). Moscow. 1958. P. 29.

[316] *Ibid*. P. 29.

The Treaty of Aigun did not contain any articles about the settlements, consular jurisdiction or trade benefits of the Russian citizens within Chinese territory, i.e., the major conditions typical of the treaties with semi-colonial countries. Moreover, by retaining China's jurisdiction over the Manchu and Chinese population on the left-side of the Amur River's basin, the Treaty of Aigun, to some extent, infringed upon the interests of Russia.

During the signing of the Treaty of Aigun, Ye. Putyatin -- sent to China to negotiate other matters -- was in Tientsin. Putyatin, being a mediator between the Qing officials and Western powers and not aware of the successful outcome of the negotiations in Aigun, signed the Treaty of Tientsin with Qing representatives who felt impelled to set a precisely defined border in several areas between the two states.[317]

Only with the Treaty of Tientsin, Russia obtained the rights of the most-favored nation as stipulated for Western powers in the Sino-British Nanking Treaty of 1842 and the Sino-British Corollary Agreement of 1843; thus the rights and benefits that were obtained by other powers were to be extended to Russia as well. The Treaty of Tientsin also contained other provisions that did not infringe upon China's sovereignty -- for example, Article 2 stipulated parity between Russia and China in diplomatic relations.[318]

It should be made clear in this context that the usual pattern of international communication in the past did not constitute signing treaties concerning every single problem which arose in bilateral relations (which would have allowed for a less subjective discussion about the "inequity" for certain countries in bilateral relations), but rather to incorporate all bilateral issues in the same document. Thus the provisions pertaining, for example, to the border demarcation -- even when it referred to the traditional historical borders that were not disputed by the counteragent country -- happened to be included in the general treaty where the other provisions were or could be of unequal nature.

In 1860, N.P. Ignatiev, the Russian envoy, and Prince Gong, the Qing authorized representative, signed the Corollary Treaty of Peking. This treaty confirmed the provisions of the Treaty of Aigun and recognized the Ussuri Territory (the Maritime Territory) -- formerly a joint possession -- as being within the Russian domain. The Treaty of Peking put into effect

---

[317] A.N. Khokhlov. "The Putyatin - Qi Ying Negotiations in 1858". *10th Academic Conference "State and Society in China"*. Vol. 2. Moscow. 1979.

[318] *Russko-Kitaiiskiye Otnosheniya. 1689-1916. Ofitsialniye Documenty.* (Russian-Chinese Relations. 1689-1916. Official Documents). P. 31.

the demarcation of the border in those areas of the Far East which, in view of the Russian diplomats and according to the treaties, had remained undemarcated, i.e., those territories which were left "in the common possession" of both states until this demarcation.[319]

The Treaty of Peking defined the Eastern (Article 1) and Western (Article 2) sections of the Russian Chinese border, outlined in general terms the border in Central Asia and defined the order of resolution of border incidents as well as the regulations for trade between Russia and China.[320] The Russian government was allowed to station Consuls in Urga and Kyakhta, while the Qing government could send its Consuls to the capital and other cities of Russia.

Like the Treaty of Tientsin, the Treaty of Peking also provided new benefits for the Russian citizens. However, as seen by contemporary Russian historians, the "territorial" articles of the Treaty of Peking still cannot be considered unequal, since Russia reobtained Amuria and annexed the lands that prior to the new demarcation formally had been in the "common" domain, not populated by the Han Chinese and administratively not subordinated to the Qing Empire.[321]

The reapprochment between Russia and the Qing Empire in Central Asia during the mid-19th century resulted in the necessity of demarcating the border in that region as well. Since the Treaty of Peking provided only a general outline of the border in Central Asia, in 1861 the two sides entered negotiations aimed at more detailed demarcations. The talks were completed on September 25, 1864 when the Chuguchak (Tachen) Protocol on the state border from Altai to Pamir was signed, specifying the border with due consideration to the natural boundaries. The agreements were arrived at from the real correlation of forces and from the military *status-quo*; the borderline was determined through diplomatic efforts rather than military confrontation.

On February 12, 1881 Russia and China signed the St. Petersburg (or Ili) Treaty by which Russia agreed with the restoration of Chinese sovereignty in the Ili Valley, minus its Western portion (with the consent of the

---

[319] *Ibid.* P.29.

[320] N. Ye. Yedinarkhova. "Trade Questions and Commercial Regime in the Sino-Russian Treaty of Peking (1860)." *Problemy Sotsialno-Ekonomicheskogo i Politicheskogo Razvitiya Stran Vostoka* (Problems of the Socio-Economic and Political Development of Oriental Countries). Irkutsk. 1981.

[321] Yu.D. Akashev. "The Amurian Question and its Reflection by Russian Periodicals in the 19th Century". *Obschestvennaya Problematika Periodicheskoi Pechati Rossii* (19th - Nach. 20th V.V.). (The Social Problematic in Russian Journals. 19th - Early 20th Centuries). Moscow. 1989; Ye. L. Besprozvannikh. *Priamuriye v Sisteme Russko-Kitaiskikh Otnoshenii*. (Near-Amuria in the System of Sino-Russian Relations in the 17th - Mid-19th Centuries). Moscow. 1983; 2nd edition. Khabarovsk. 1986.

Chinese government, the Ili Valley had been occupied by the Russian army in 1871 to control the local population, which had actually overthrown the Qing authorities in Xinjiang, in order to regain the border stability). The western portion of the Ili valley as well as the Russian lands as such were designated by the Treaty of St. Petersburg for the settlement of local residents who willingly adopted Russian citizenship after the restoration of Chinese jurisdiction over the rest of the Ili territory. Besides this, the Treaty of St. Petersburg determined trade relations between Russia and China and its "territorial" articles actually defined the current Chinese border with Russia and the newly independent states of Central Asia.[322] As for the Pamirs, the demarcation was put into effect only through the exchange of diplomatic notes in 1894, when the two sides agreed "to retain their mutual positions" in the Pamirs along the Sarykol Range.[323] That line is still in effect today.

So, for more than three centuries, the two empires were engaged in the complex process of developing their contacts, which were primarily concerned with the opening and settlement of trade and border issues.

It was the growth of Tsarist Russian Empire -- which incorporated Siberia, the Far East, and then Kazakhstan and Central Asia -- on the one hand, and the development of the Manchu Empire of Qing -- that ruled China, and then incorporated Korea, Northern Manchuria, a part of the Amuria, Mongolia (East, South, and then North), the Dzungar Khanate, and Eastern Turkestan -- on the other hand, that led the states to the rapprochement and the demarcation of their common border.

In this light, a discussion of these processes should be aimed at an analysis of other aspects of the relationship. It is not only the "aggression" and the "territorial acquisition," or the "colonizing" and "economic" activities of the two states which matters so much, even though these notions do have a right to exist as far as they describe the same phenomena but seen through the interests of different states. It seems more important to discuss the general laws of interaction between these two civilizations (Asian and Western [or more precisely non-Asian], Confucian and Christian) for which it seems hardly possible to apply the simple dichotomy of "equity or inequity." In their basic dimensions, such laws have been determined by the retrospectively observable communication between an economically and socially dynamic capitalist empire and its decrepiting

---

[322] A. D. Voskressenski "The Ili Crisis" in the Sino-Russian Relations: New Time - New Estimations". *Novoye v Izuchenii Kitaya* (New Concepts in Chinese Studies). Vol. 5. Moscow. 1990.

[323] See "Agreements between Russia and China on Borders and on Border Affairs". *Izvestiya Ministerstva Inostrannykh Del* (Newsletter of the Foreign Ministry). Vol. 4. Petrograd. 1914. P. 56-63.

semi-feudal counterpart; these two empires were engaged in interaction within territories that formally did not belong to either of them but were vitally important for both in terms of their respective state and national interests. This resulted in the situation becoming so tense that even more suffering were brought upon not only these two giant-neighbors but also upon the indigenous peoples of those territories which were either at the stage of corruption of their tribal systems (such as in southern Siberia, Transbaikalia, northern Manchuria, Amuria, or the Maritime territory) or at various stages of nomadic feudalism (such as in Mongolia, the Dzungar Khanate, Western and Eastern Turkestan, or the Kazakh khanates). But the objective mechanism for the formation of state borders during the period was such that it is only in a relative sense that the contemporary concepts of morality and ethics could be applied to these past developments. The latter cannot be considered by historians in isolation from the social phenomena and cruel habits of that epoch. And, being connected with the concepts of national security, the issue is certainly timely and naturally attracts equal attention on both sides of the border today.

Evidently, the elements of inequity can be traced to both sides, since both empires carried out a colonial policy while their separate state interests, marked by the subjective interpretation of the reality, were quite often at conflict. The Qings started with attempts to treat Russia as a vassal state; they exerted pressure upon the Russian ambassador at Nerchinsk, refused to provide the same rights to Russian merchants as those granted to Chinese traders in Russia, etc. It was only in the mid-19th century that the elements of inequity appeared in Russian policy vis-à-vis China. Unlike the Qing, however, Russia initially strived to enter fully equal relations with China. However, while the elements of inequity did not constitute the entire character of the Sino-Russian relationship, it should be realized that this understanding does not at all reject the fact that the Tsarist government unfairly treated China during certain historical periods.

Since then, while many historical events have marked Sino-Russian relations, peace has prevailed in the almost 300 years of ties between the two neighbors: Russia and China have never been in a state of formally declared war, and in principle (a rare case in history!) have always managed to solve their problems through diplomatic negotiations.

In the mid 1890s, the Sino-Russian relationship entered a new phase which was qualitatively different from previous phases. What constituted the primary difference was the advent of Imperialism in Russia. The center of gravity in the Sino-Russian relationship shifted to Russia's colonial and economic infiltration of China. As seen by the Tsarist strategists of that time, Russia's state interests could only be realized by having adjacent territories interconnected thus creating a "buffer zone," controlled by Russians. Simultaneously, however, Tsarist Russia's policy toward China was in many ways different from that of Britain, France, Germany, or Japan. Russia's primary interest was to preserve China as a united, independent and friendly neighbor.[324] Following China's defeat in the Sino-Japanese war, the Russian envoy, together with France and Germany, urged Japan to relinquish its annexation of the Liaodong Peninsula and to reduce the retribution demanded from China by one third. At the same time, the Russian government organized a loan through Russian and French banks worth one hundred million rubles, which was provided on conditions that were quite beneficial for China.

In 1896, Russia and China, "willing to capitalize upon their peaceful relations... and to protect the Asian continent against a new foreign invasion," (Preamble)[325] entered a military alliance against Japan. But, as a result of the treaty, Russia also obtained the opportunity to build the Chinese Eastern Railway along with the right of free transportation and the respective "belt of alienation."

Soon after that, the Tsarist army together with the troops of seven other nations took part in the suppression of *Yihetuan* rebellion (the so-called "Boxer Uprising"). As a result, China was committed to the payment of indemnity worth 450 million silver *liangs* (taels) to those nations which took part in the suppression of the rebellion, including Russia. Despite this, however, when the Japanese government invited Russia to act in concert with Japan in the suppression of the Republican Revolution of 1911, the Russian government refused.

The Revolution of 1917 in Russia marked the beginning of a new and complicated phase in Sino-Russian relations. The first decree of the Soviet Government - the Decree of Peace - formally annulled the secret treaties that had determined Russia's preferential rights in the countries of the Far East. The speech by the People's Commissar for Foreign Affairs, G.V. Chicherin, at the 5th Congress of the Soviets, the Address of the RSFSR Soviet of People's Commissars to the Chinese people and the governments of southern and northern China of July 25, 1919, and the Note of the People's Commissariat for Foreign Affairs to the Chinese Government on September 27, 1920 -- all clearly formulated the elements of the former Sino-Russian relationship being abrogated by the Soviet state. The Soviet government nullified the Russian-Chinese Treaty of 1896, the Peking Protocol

---

[324] It was totally contradictory to the later Stalin's course toward China.

[325] *Russko-Kitaiskiye Otnosheniya. 1689-1916. Ofitsialniye Dokumenty* (Russian-Chinese Relations. 1689-1916. Official Documents). P. 73.

of 1901, and all agreements with Japan from 1907 to 1916; it also gave up the annexation of Manchuria, the Russian share of the so-called "Boxers' indemnity," the extraterritorial rights and the concessions.

So, except specific treaties -- which were eliminated by the Soviet government, "by which the Tsarist government, together with its allies, and through violence and bribery subjugated the peoples of the Orient and, mainly, the Chinese people to provide benefits for the Russian capitalists, landlords, and generals"[326] -- Russia meant to abrogate not the treaties as a whole, as was stressed by some Chinese researchers, but rather the provisions in those treaties which placed China in an unfair position and that were listed in the mentioned documents. Such an approach corresponded to the principles of foreign policy as formulated by V.I. Lenin, the first head of the Soviet state, at the Second All-Russia Congress of Soviets. He said that the plundering governments of the West not only agreed about the pillage; among those provisions they placed other points pertaining to good-neighborly relations. In Lenin's view, all provisions pertaining to plunder and violence should be nullified, while those which pertained to friendly relations and economic agreement should be left alone.[327] Interestingly enough, this approach actually is the basis for the Russian Federation's position toward these Sino-Russian treaties of the past. The legacy of this approach was heavily disputed in the past both by Guomindang and Communist authorities in China.

So, the relationship between Russia and China up to the end of the 19th century consisted of:

1. The specifics of all Sino-Russian treaties which contained both "equal" and "unequal" articles thus making it impossible to analyze any treaty in general with the intent of declaring it "equal" or "unequal";
2. The special character of Sino-Russian relations which can be explained through the objective laws of intercivilization interaction within the modernizational processes that took place between the economically and socially dynamic capitalist Russian Empire and the decrepiting semi-feudal Qing Empire, and occurred within those adjacent territories which formally did not belong to either country though the possession of them --

---

[326] *Sovetsko-Kitayskiye Otnosheniya. 1917-1957. Sbornik Dokumentov.* (The Sino-Soviet Relations. 1917-1957. Collected Documents). Moscow. 1959. P. 44.

[327] V.I. Lenin. "Concluding Remarks on the Report on Peace of October 28/ November 8". *Polnoye Sobraniye Sochinenii.* (Completed Collected Works). Moscow. 1958-1965. Vol. 35. P. 20.

whether direct (through jurisdiction) or indirect (through a sphere of influence) -- affected the state interests of both countries;
3. And, the Russian strategy for the preservation of a friendly and hence, united China, as well as the emphasis on trade as the top priority meeting the national interests of both countries.

The national interests of both Russia and China required security and peaceful conditions for development, sovereignty, and territorial integrity -- naturally, these categories of international law were understood in a somewhat different way in the past. However, the fact that these two nations have never entered into a state of officially announced hostilities reflects those basic interests. However, the state interests of Russia and China did not always coincide and, during some periods of history, were in conflict. This is because the smaller components of the state's interests, such as the class, group, personal, *et al.* interests, being under the strong influence of subjective factors, could be in contradiction. This fact predetermined the changes (sometimes, quite radical) in Russian policy as compared to its long-term strategic course of seeking friendly relations with China, as well as the shifts in the Qing Empire's foreign policy (in particular, their transition from the earlier "expansion of the Empire's borders" and the creation of the "buffer zones" to their later "isolationist" policy).

In the mid-1890s the center of gravity in the Sino-Russian relationship shifted to Russia's political and economic infiltration of China. However, the people of Russia are not to be blamed for this course, which was realized irrespectively of the people's opinion. As the renown Russian historian M.I. Karamzin said, history retains bad memories, indeed. The Russian people paid for that policy due to the lack of their own rights and the hostility of those who saw them as "aggressors."

SINO-SOVIET AND SINO-RUSSIAN BORDER RELATIONS: FROM PAST TO PRESENT

The questions discussed in the previous sections seem to be of a purely scholarly character, i.e., irrelevant to the current political situation between both of the countries. Unfortunately, recent history proves that is wholly incorrect. The border dispute, based on ideological divergences as well as on historical roots of instability in the region, has been one of the most crucial questions in Sino-Soviet relations for over 40 years.

The collapse of the USSR and the emergence of new political dilemmas would seem to indicate that the border issue would be pushed to the side. But after some rather careless statements made by Mr. Yeltsin shortly after the creation of the Russian Federation concerning the necessity of reconsidering the frontiers between the former republics and Russia, it became evident that border questions, the most sensitive in interstate relations, would not only emerge and, perhaps, even more sharply than in the past after some time, but could not be handled by nonprofessionals. In this sense, the latest of the secret agreements between the former USSR and China concerning their borders allows for some breathing-room in the longest running negotiations ever undertaken between such immense nations, and concerning a border which is considered the longest in the world and even appears in the *Guiness Book of World Records*.

These questions will seem to be even more urgent in the future since all frontier problems in Russia eventually become cross-pollinated -- the uncertainty of its western borders with Europe, of its borders with the former Soviet republics, of the rise in nationalism, and of the borders of autonomous republics within Russia (some of which have hinted that they have independent historical traditions connected with the history, perhaps not of China itself, but with some regions of China). Another warning sign should be the rise in Islamic fundamentalism which has been witnessed in various former Soviet republics and provinces in China, and which perhaps aspires to reconstruct the former Muslim empire, though in a different form. And even the uncertainties of the so-called Northern territories, disputed by Russia and Japan, is connected with the question. And while those concerned with a particular border issue zealously watch the developments of other issues, even the smallest precedent within one of the issues as mentioned above could set off a chain of destabilizing factors. The most dangerous of these destabilizing factors, without any doubt, would be the former Sino-Soviet border. This enormous border has been one of the majors factors (though not the only, of course) in bringing Russia and China to the brink of war more than once. And although these two giants are now preoccupied with internal problems and a repeat of the "Great Polemics" seems more problematic now as leaders begin to realize that when playing "Big Games" nobody wins, the border question in Central Asia remains unresolved. In fact, the border question in Central Asia will continue to remain unresolved since the form in which these new nations and Russia interact remains unknown. It is also obvious that Chinese Communism has been and will be influenced by the collapse of the Soviet model, and despite economic victories, is on the threshold of uneasy times with hardly predictable consequences for the Chinese empire itself. Such consequences could perhaps even lead to the disintegration of the current Chinese state and the emergence of a new order in Asia which will be more unwieldy.

It is perhaps preferable to briefly look over the history of Sino-Soviet border relations within the last few years to understand the present situation. This should be done especially in view of the recently sharp polemics between Russia and China concerning border issues and the historical origins of border territories.

The Sino-Soviet border, which has remained generally intact up till this day, was formed decades ago while considering the natural boundaries present and the large number of Sino-Russian treaties drawn up in the past. These historical Sino-Russian treaties still form the juridical basis of the border.

During the first years of the Sino-Soviet relationship, the border between the two states was considered as a border between two good neighbors. Accordingly, due to the Treaty of Friendship, Union and Mutual Assistance, signed between the USSR and China in 1950, the population of the border regions maintained active ties and pursued commerical and cultural exchanges. The two sides attempted to resolve diverse questions, which concerned, as usual, the border of the two states, in an atmosphere of mutual understanding. In fact, a package of documents on the border issues had been signed among the large number of treaties and agreements concerning different aspects of Sino-Soviet ties (in particular, on the *cooperation* between the two states in this area on such matters as the normal navigability of the border rivers, and on the development of the timber industry within the border areas, etc.)[328].

Throughout the initial years of the Sino-Soviet relationship, the leaders of the two states did not proclaim the existence of any territorial disputes between China and the Soviet Union, i.e., there were no official doubts about the legitimacy or the correctness of the border. Nevertheless, the situation even then did not seem as clear as it has been represented in the Soviet scholarly literature on the theme, which has tried to prove that this period was the "golden years" of Sino-Soviet relations. It is known that for a very short period of time, Chinese scholarly literature, as well, strongly emphasized the friendly relations between the two states. The reality, however, is that during these years, the ideological proximity of the two governing Communist parties forced the leaders to pretend to forget about the lack of clarity on the border issue and to present a situation where the state interests of the two countries coincided to an international audience.

This condition of forced cooperation was also brought about by the perception that China and Russia's surrounding neighbors were "capitalist and hostile," and by an era of military tension brought on by the Cold War, especially exemplified for China by the potential threat for invasion by Chian Kai-shek's army and the possibility of an economic blockade and political isolation led by the USA. That is why the Chinese leaders at the time repeatedly underlined the fact that after the October Revolution, the Soviet Union pursued a relationship with China based on equality and respect for the sovereign rights of the Chinese people. For example, in 1945, when addressing the Seventh Congress of the Communist Party of China, Mao Zedong stressed the fact that the Soviet Union was the first state in the world which nullified all former "unequal treaties" with China and signed new, "equal" ones. This was also emphasized by Mao during his visit to Moscow on December 16, 1949.[329] It has be said that Chairman Mao yielded to Stalin's pressure, but it does not seem so because Mao was

---

[328] For reference see O.B.Borisov and B.T.Koloskov. *Soviet-Chinese Relations, 1945-1970*. Bloomington. Indiana University Press. 1975 - the book, written by the two top Communist party experts on Sino-Soviet relations, gives an excellent example of the 'pure' Soviet understanding of the problems of the split - unfortunately the only special monograph on Sino-Soviet relations written by Russians till now, and published both in Russian and English.

[329] *Pravda*. 03.30.1969.

the only person among the "leaders of the new world" at the time who really did not recognize Stalin as the "great proletarian leader of all times and all nations." The notion that, at the time, China had entered into the "Big Game" also does not seem very probable -- this phenomenon has only occurred more recently.

At the beginning of the 1950s, the Soviet Union, responding to a Chinese request, had provided for China a number of topographical maps in which the entire border was shown. It was later stressed in the Statement of the Government of the USSR, on March 29, 1960, in this connection, that "Chinese authorities at the time did not make any observations or complaints concerning the presentation of the border shown in these maps, and the border has thus been in place."[330] When signing, in 1951, an agreement on the navigation rules of the border rivers and the Khanka Lake, as well as an agreement concerning the mutual fighting of future forest fires, it is probable that both the Soviet and Chinese authorities took into consideration the border lines which were drawn up on these topographical maps.

Between 1956 and 1959, many cases of border violations occurred, revealing an obvious sign that something was wrong in connection with this issue. The border authorities tried, and succeeded at first, to resolve border questions without interference from the central governments, thus providing a false impression (especially for the Soviet leaders) that this question could be resolved locally.

One may argue about the real intentions of the Soviet Union, but in reality the USSR promised China and other countries, at the time, to conclude an agreement on border procedures and mutual assistance in regulating frontier problems. The Soviet authorities of the time claimed that they were thinking of how to strengthen friendly relations. This description of the facts, however, was not even accepted by China in the context of the understanding the divergences between the interests of their two states.

Border violations along the Sino-Soviet border became even more severe in the 1960s. To prevent an increase of friction within the border area (but in reality to prevent the deepening of state discrepancies), the Soviet government declared in May 1963 its readiness to hold consultations on a more precise definition of the border within those areas where the border line was in a redemarcation process.

---

[330] *Ibid.* The Chinese maps with the new border line, different from that of the Soviet variant, were made available to the Soviet side by the Chinese counterpart only in 1964.

The consultations between the Soviet and Chinese delegations on a governmental level were held in Beijing from February 25 to August 22, 1964. It is very important to note that while the Soviet side considered this diplomatic process as consultations, the Chinese considered them as actual border negotiations. This different understanding of the character of the diplomatic activity from the beginning could only hinder an overall mutual understanding. The border negotiations, having been held in an atmosphere of normal and friendly relations, presented an opportunity to define, through mutual consent, the border line in various disputed areas within a very short time. The two sides, however, only believed in theory that the successful end of the negotiation process would benefit friendly relations between the Soviet and Chinese people. The quick resolution of the border question corresponded only with the national interests of the two countries, i.e., with the interests of the Russian and Chinese people, but not with the state (government) interests (i.e., not with the USSR or the PRC) in the highly subjective understanding of the diplomatic strategists at the time.

The beginning of ideological polemics between the Communist Party of the Soviet Union and the Communist Party of China led to the aggravation of interstate discrepancies, and the Beijing negotiations ended without any result. Nevertheless, the two sides achieved an agreement to continue the negotiations in Moscow on October 1964. Unfortunately this new round was not held in 1964, because the leaders were preoccupied by their ideological split.

Little by little, the strategic confrontation between the USSR and China acquired a global character, and during Brezhnev's era the militarization of the Sino-Soviet conflict occurred. This, in turn, lead to military confrontation, some causes of which, of course, were the failure of the Sino-Soviet border negotiations in 1964, as well as a statement made by Chairman Mao, considered by the Soviet side as a claim for 1.5 million square kilometers of Soviet territory.[331] But if the real position of the Chinese leadership was properly analyzed, it could be seen that the Statement of the Chinese Government [October 8, 1969], especially stressed that "China does not request the return of the territories torn away by Tsarist Russia through these [i.e., Sino-Russian] treaties.[332]" But this key phrase

---

[331] Other real origins of the split, without any ideological shelter for the Soviet side, have been analyzed in Russia by S.Goncharov. See: S. Goncharov. "From Union through Hostility to Good-Neighborly Relations. The 40 Years of Sino-Soviet Relations". *Literaturnaya Gazeta*. #40. 10.04.1989.

[332] *The Statement of the Chinese Government*. 10.08.1969. Beijing. Foreign Language Press. 1969. I have used my own translation for the version of the statement in Chinese. Very similar formulas can also be seen in other Statements of the Chinese Government (05.24.1969; 07.07.1969).

has not been considered by Soviet analysts (they may have not wanted to see it, considering the existing interstate relations through the ideological split).[333] As the interstate conflict became even more severe, any Chinese scholarly publication or information which was presented by the Chinese media was considered by the Soviet side as "a scholarly basis" for research into Chinese "territorial claims." This position, held by the apparatchiks in the Central Committee of the CPSU, inspired a series of critical publications by some Soviet scholars, including many articles and books which dramatically emphasized the confrontation. This occurred as well among Chinese scholars, who tried to prove that Soviet foreign policy was "the continuation of Tsarist Russia's aggression." In rebuttal, the Soviet scholars maintained that China "claimed some parts of Soviet territory," and that "China was continuing its strategy of expansion pursued by the Chinese emperors." Thus the abstract ideological divergences were made "understandable" to the common people.

In this particular case, what really aggravated the situation was that the frontier, which was drawn up based upon natural boundaries, did not coincide with the historical borders of the ethnic communities. This type of border, in principle, could become a zone for potential tension during periods of confrontation or instability. This could especially occur when border changes in the past have been occurred either by expansion or by the arbitrariness of the authorities.

The agreement on the resumption of the Soviet-Chinese Negotiations on the Settlement of Border Questions (the official title of the negotiations) was held only on September 11, 1969 during a meeting of the Chairman of the USSR's Soviet Ministers Kosygin and the Premier of the State Council of China Zhou Enlai, in Beijing. The two sides came to the conclusion that they should try to find a way to thwart the escalation of the conflict, especially in such a touchy sphere as border relations. Unfortunately such a conclusion was made only after sanguinary clashes near the island of Damanskyi and the small town of Zhalanashkol (in the Semipalatinskaya oblast in Central Asia).

---

[333] The split gave a short term benefit for Soviet sinology - for the first time the leaders of the state began to understand that the case of such a huge neighbor as China, with its own particular historical traditions not similar to those of Russia, could not be dealt with by non-professionals. At the same time, during the split, a large number of "specialists" on China emerged, who tried to make careers out of the split, producing research and prognosis, which had nothing to do with social sciences. Thus, the long term consequences for Russian sinology were created, because this discipline emerged only through the ideological split. Thus, in the Russian Federation new possibilities with unpredictable consequences were created by the use of non-professionals in the field of the Sino-Russian relations.

Terrified by the prospect of possible war, (it seemed obvious that the conflict became uncontrollable at the time) the heads of state in both the USSR and China expressed with a single will that the two delegations, beginning new negotiations, should be led by such basic principles as: The neccessity to settle border questions based on Sino-Russian treaties which had remained in effect up till the time; and, that the two sides have no territorial claims on each other and would strictly maintain the status-quo concerning the border. The rather similar positions on basic principles could theoretically create essential conditions for propitious prospects. However, during the meeting of the two heads of state other problems arose, which in turn provoked differences of opinions on the border issue.

The two states only expressed their views concerning the border questions, and stopped short of actually committing themselves to any obligations. Because each side understood the results of the negotiations only according to their subjective state interests, unofficial polemics on how to properly consider these results began soon after the meeting.

Neither during the above-mentioned meeting, nor in the forthcoming correspondence between the leadership concerning the character of Sino-Soviet relations and border problems was a consensus achieved. The Soviets stressed that since these regions were considered as "disputed" only by the Chinese and not by themselves, these areas could not be considered as "disputed" according to international law. Consequently, according to this theory, the two sides could negotiate only on a more precise definition of the border in various regions, and so the diplomatic process between the two states should actually be considered consultations on the border issue, and not negotiations. It was natural that such casuistic definition could not meet the understanding of the Chinese counterparts. The admission of so-called "disputed" border regions, can endanger, as Soviet officials understood it, the legitimacy of the entire border, and could even give rise to questions concerning the Soviet border with Europe and sharpen polemics with Japan. Consequently, it would make the position of Soviet authority even more vulnerable than before.

These divergent perceptions concerning the actual purpose of the negotiations were the root causes in the impossibility in reaching even a preliminary agreement on military personnel, guard posting and the form economic activity would take within the "disputed" regions. It meant, in effect, that the two sides could not even create the prerequisites to stabilize the situation. The Soviet Union and China also did not stipulate the necessity to achieve an agreement on maintaining the status-quo of the frontier before considering the border issues, due to their different interpretations of the concept of "status-quo," relying again upon their subjective understanding of the negotiations' main item.

Simultaneously, analysts on both states understood that these divergences should not result in a permanent impediment to future negotiations; it is only through negotiations that both sides could bring their positions closer to a consensus. That is why the Soviet and Chinese governments decided to renew negotiations on the border issue on October 20, 1969, in Beijing. However, the presence of these differences thwarted the successful conclusion of these discussions on the frontier issue at the time.

The revival of border negotiations in 1987 can be considered as the most important event of that year in Sino-Soviet relations, reflecting new trends in interstate relations. The new rounds in the negotiation process were held in a pragmatic atmosphere for the first time in the last twenty-seven years, and were considered very important for both sides because they could, in principle, improve bilateral relations, thus freeing both countries to resolve their internal problems. During the first round of negotiations, the two sides agreed to reconsider the demarcation of the whole border, beginning from its eastern sector (i.e., from Lake Khanka to the Mongolian part of the border near the sources of the Argun River).[334] During the second round of negotiations, the two sides discussed questions relating to the precise demarcation of the eastern sector of the border. Both the Soviets and the Chinese expressed a uniform opinion concerning the rationality of the border issues' decision, relying upon past Sino-Russian and Sino-Soviet treaties, and considering the modern border in accordance with the international principles of borders on navigable rivers -- through a fairway, and on the nonnavigable ones -- through the middle of the river or its main arm.

Both sides also agreed that, while continuing the negotiation process on the governmental level, a so-called "working group" of experts would also be organized. This working group would analyze the concrete questions of border line demarcation on the whole of the eastern sector.[335]

During the regular rounds in 1988, both sides finished the work concerning the eastern sector and proceeded to the consideration of the western sector (i.e., the Central Asian part of the Sino-Soviet border from Mongolia to the Pamirs).

It is natural that throughout the political situation shortly preceding the collapse of the USSR, both sides paid careful attention to the resolution of border problems. Soviet authorities were trying to settle all exter-

---

[334] *Pravda*, 01.24.1987.
[335] *Pravda*, 08.22.1987.

nal problems to concentrate on the lack of political stability inside the country, while the Chinese were afraid of losing the USSR as a socialist state in view of the uncertainty concerning those authorities that can sign border agreements. During the meetings between the heads of the delegations (i.e. between Igor Rogachev,[336] Deputy Foreign Minister of Russia and the Chinese Minister of Foreign Affairs, Wu Xueqian), which were held in 1987, and after the end of the second round of negotiations, the unanimous opinion was expressed that the settlement of the Sino-Soviet border question and the transformation of the frontier into a zone of peace and good-neighbors could have great importance in the future not only for both sides but for the preservation of peace and stability in all of Asia[337].

Soviet Foreign Minister Edward Shevardnadze, answering questions being asked by the TASS news agency after the negotiations with his Chinese counterpart Qian Qichen, emphasized at the time that the solution in decreasing military confrontation and military buildup on the border and to implement the "measures of faith" was related to the new military doctrine of the state, which would be strictly defensive in character.

During their meeting, the two ministers decided to discuss the border question at the highest level, having in mind the goal to achieve a peaceful and friendly atmosphere on the border.[338] Analyzing its new conception of border relations, the Soviet side stressed a different approach in principle, the main idea of which is that the overall military dimension could not be considered as an aspect of international politics; military presence should be limited only within national boundaries.

Analyzing the prospects of Sino-Soviets relations shortly before the Soviet-Chinese summit meeting researchers in the Kennan Institute of Advanced Russian Studies (The Woodrow Wilson Center) R. Menon and D. Abele correctly stressed:

> "Conditions for settlement of the Sino-Soviet border dispute now are in marked contrast from the 1960s when the Brezhnev military buildup was in full swing, Sino-Soviet political polemics were intense, and tensions exploded into military confrontations along the Ussuri River. The improvement of Sino-Soviet relations, due in great part to the reform-minded leadership in both countries, has resulted in a decrease of border tensions and mutual security concerns. In such an environment, both

---

[336] Currently the Russian Ambassador to China.
[337] *Pravda*, 08.18.1987.
[338] *Izvestia*, 12.04.1988.

sides should see the benefit in making compromises that will strengthen security in the region and establish an atmosphere of cooperation.

"In a very real sense, however, the Sino-Soviet border still represents to the Soviet military a thin line between a growing, heavily-populated geopolitical rival to the south and a sparsely populated, mineral-rich expanse of the Soviet empire far from the heart of the homeland. Given the objective of protecting Khabarovsk, Vladivostok, and the Trans-Siberian Railway, which are all close to the Sino- Soviet border, Soviet border forces are the first and the last line of defence with no buffer territory in which to retreat. Soviet strategic concerns seemingly argue against border concessions that would increase the vulnerability of Soviet cities, communication links and military installations.

"Soviet political leaders will have to weigh the cautionary advice of the Soviet military against the prospects for a comprehensive detente with China. A Soviet rapprochement with China is a critical step that could open diplomatic and trade opportunities for the Soviet Union in Asia and help create an atmosphere of confidence and security in the area. Given the Soviet commitment to "new thinking," the advantages of the detente with China, and Soviet economic pressure to reduce defence spending, Moscow may ask whether security concerns in east Asia have become less salient, and if so, whether it is possible to accommodate Chinese territorial claims."[339]

The changes in the positions of both sides, when approaching one another, created conditions for the May 1989 summit meeting, which was held in Beijing. After the meeting, the two sides published *A Joint Communique* (May 18, 1989), which constituted the political basis for Sino-Soviet relations. This basis for bilateral relations became the easily realizable correlation between national and state interests, which were grounded on the universal principles of international relations and peaceful coexistence.[340]

Both sides went on from the point where normalization of bilateral relations should not be oriented against any third country or should not hurt any country's interests and must follow modern trends of international development.The USSR and China agreed on the primary goal -- to cut military forces in the Sino-Soviet border region down to a minimal level, stressing that the border issue should be resolved fairly and rationally based on past Sino-Russian treaties, with the generally accepted

---

[339] R. Menon. D. Abele. "Security Dimensions of Soviet Territorial Disputes with China and Japan". *Journal of Northeast Asian Studies*. Spring 1989. Vol. YIII, #1. P. 16-17.

[340] Both sides could not reach a unified agreement on the meaning of the principles of peaceful coexistence: the Soviet side insisted on "universal principles" (!) and the Chinese stressed the "five principles" (!) though the difference in reality did not seem very obvious.

rules of the international law and through equal consultations in an atmosphere of mutual understanding and mutual pliancy. Thus, the nonconfrontational approach has become a dominant theme in modern times.

Both sides also have agreed to create an "efficient negotiation mechanism." During the summit meeting the Soviets and Chinese also thoroughly discussed how the border settlement was proceeding, and decided that the most important questions would be discussed by the actual foreign ministers to provide a new impetus for the process.

It is acknowledged that the stage of waiting and theoretical discussion has ended and the process of practical realization of the proclaimed objectives has begun. Both sides have created joint groups of military and diplomatic experts to pursue an earnest discussion; it has been in this way that real achievements have been realized throughout the past several years. At the end of 1990, nine-tenths of the entire Sino-Russian border was considered and approved. The joint group for the juridicial registration of the approved sector of the border,[341] began the work in October 1990. The topographical map group began the work in December of the same year.[342]

The strengthening of the so-called "measures of faith" in the military field has become an important landmark in the border settlement. Negotiations on the mutual reduction of military forces in border areas began at the end of 1989. In October 1989, the Chief of the Soviet General Staff Moiseev emphasized his intentions to liquidate practically all Soviet fighting detachments quartered along the Sino-Soviet border. Apart from the withdrawal of Soviet forces from Mongolia, he underscored his intention of reducing the number of military personnel in three military areas: Zabaikalskyi, Dalnevostochnyi and Turkestanskyi, which are all close to the border.[343] During the visit of the Chinese Premier Li Pen to the Soviet Union in April 1990, the foreign ministers of both countries signed a special agreement concerning the leading principles of the reduction of military forces and the strengthening of the "measures of faith" in the military field on the border areas.

Not long before its collapse, the USSR began the process of a unilateral reduction of its military forces in the Asian-Pacific theater, which of course was an important stabilizing prerequisite for a border settlement in the Asian part of the former USSR. The Soviet authorities have come to

---

[341] *Izvestia*, 12.04.1988.

[342] *Izvestia*, 12.30.1990.

[343] *Mezdunarodnaya zhizn*, #10, 1989.

understand that this sort of action was not a simple caprice of its neighbors.

In January 1990, it was announced that the Soviet military group in the Far East theater would be reduced by 120 thousand soldiers; 16 military ships would be cut from the Pacific Ocean Fleet. The air forces in this region would also be reduced. The former General Staff intended to withdraw 75% of the Soviet land forces from Mongolia and all of the air forces. This would have been not less then fifty thousand soldiers and personnel. Soviet military authorities confirmed their readiness to remove, in accordance with the wishes of Mongolia, all former Soviet troops stationed in Mongolia.

Simultaneously the structural reorganization of Soviet military forces in the border region had begun. The goal of this reorganization still is: first, to transform the character of the military detachments from offensive to defensive so that at the second stage to achieve full demilitarization[344] of the border. The only question for the new Russian state now is how to put all these plans into effect in the poorly assimilated areas of Siberia while the central regions experience the inevitable pains of mass unemployment from future market reforms which would invariably make the demilitarization process only more difficult.

Nevertheless, although well-intentioned all these planned measures are insufficient since the way out of the current border deadlock can be found only in introducing a new conception of border relations. This is the only way to ensure progressive movement on both countries. According to some estimates, the former Soviet Union alone, spent from 200 up to 300 billion rubles (at the old rates) to ensure a military presence in the Sino-Soviet border region.[345] This can be considered a classic example of how an inefficient foreign policy can only contribute to the collapse of any regime.

During an official visit to the USSR by the General Secretary of the CPC and the Chairman of the PRC's Military Council, Ziang Zeming in May 1991, both sides ascertained that positive shifts had occurred during the border negotiations. They stressed the necessity to secure the results of this shift in legal judicial form. During the summit meeting in Moscow, both sides welcomed the newly signed agreement on the eastern part of the Sino-Soviet border, stressing the unified will to intensify negotiations

---

[344] *Pravda*, 01.14.1991.

[345] *Pravda*, 07.05.1990;*Izvestia*, 10.17.1990.

on the nonsettled areas for a just, rational resolution of the questions on the historical borders.[346]

The secret border agreement,[347] signed in May 1991, and later ratified after the collapse of the Soviet Union by the Russian Parliament, represents a clear example of the compromise, - i.e., both sides decided to recognize what they should admit to at the present time. Others decisions, (i.e., the decisions on questions concerning the settlement for which both sides were unprepared), have been suspended "for future" consideration by strategists, hoping that it will not be themselves personally who must decide. These strategists are waiting for the future to become more clear, thus reducing political pressure on the leaders.

The signed agreement concerned the eastern sector of the former Sino-Soviet border, which although very substantial in length, was also the easiest to arrange, because it fixed the areas already correlated during the long history of negotiations, making "vacant" two regions along the border about 50 km long and of strategic importance to both states though on which a consensus could not be reached.[348] In this sense this news is sensational only because the basic agreement, prepared in the 1960s, was signed and ratified after 30 years of negotiations. Nevertheless, thus Russia really also made an important step in resolving the problem of the so-called Northern territories, showing that the country can reach agreements even on the touchiest questions if it really needs to or wants to.

During Yeltsin's visit to China in December 1992, both sides agreed on the necessity to "adopt" former Sino-Soviet agreements, and stressed that ideological divergences should not become an obstacle in developing bilateral relations. Both sides -- now that their political regimes are far from being stable -- emphasize the principle of noninterference into each other's internal affairs. The two sides have decided the choice of political line be independent from interstate relations, thus guaranteeing one nation's constraint should the ruling regime in the other country be toppled by the opposition. Russia and China also decided not to participate in any new military or political alliances aimed against one another, nor to conclude treaties with any third country that could be detrimental to the sovereignty and security of each country. Thus China received a guarantee that

---

[346] *Pravda.* 05.17.1991; *Izvestia,* 05.20.1991.

[347] I call it secret because only the fact that such agreement had been signed was mentioned by the Russian mass media. The exact terms of the agreement were considered confidential by both sides.

[348] It can be easily guessed from the comparison of Chinese and Soviet maps and from the extensive Chinese scholarly sources on the Sino-Soviet border question, that the two unresolved areas on the Eastern sector of the border are: the islands Tarabarov and Ussuriiskyi (*Heixiazi dao*, in Chinese), near Khabarovsk and the island Bolshoi on the Argun river.

any future Russian-American alliance will not be aimed against China. China is now seeing Russia as a stabilizing military force in Central Asia and the Asian-Pacific region, though also as a source of ideological perturbation. The Chinese desire to establish an alliance with the new government which has risen from the ruins of the defunct Communist regime in Russia demonstrates their anxiety that the world's liberal democracies can isolate China as the last great Communist state. The main Russian task had also become more or less clear: to stabilize the situation in the region while minimizing the military and financial burden of ensuring stability in the Russian-Chinese and Central Asian borders. During Yeltsin's visit to China, the sides signed an intergovernmental memorandum stressing the necessity to preserve the status-quo in the border region. Russia and China were planning to sign a special agreement in 1994, which aims to reduce the number of military detachments in border areas, and beginning in 2000 in making their military structures strictly defensive thus reflecting the friendly relations between the two countries.

Simultaneously both sides began the process of demarcating the eastern sector of the Sino-Russian border. The first meeting of the bilateral commission was held in Moscow between June 29 and July 9, 1992, while the second -- between September 12 and September 24, 1992, when a special document on the demarcation process of this sector was signed.

In October of the same year, Russia, China, Kazakhstan, Kyrgizstan and Tajikistan held negotiations on the western sector of the former Sino-Soviet border. During these negotiations, Russia, Kazakhstan, Kyrgizstan and Tajikistan formed a united delegation. The same was done when negotiations were held between November 9 and November 27, 1992, on the reduction of military detachments in the Central Asian region.

However, at the same time the western (i.e., Central Asian) sector of the former Sino-Soviet border seems quite less clear with more questions arising from the collapse of the USSR, the emergence of Russia as the successor of the Soviet Union and the firm readiness of the former Central Asian republics to obtain full independence. A considerable part of this border has still not been fixed even by the nonsophisticated Sino-Russian treaties of the past. It is not the one border line now, but the border between China and a number of newly independent states (former Soviet republics), which is practically uncovered in some large areas by special border documents, though the official interpretation of the ratified Sino-Russian agreement has mentioned that these documents do not provide for changes in the entire land frontier[349] which hints that nobody is ready

---

[349] Russian Daily - *Novoye Russkoye Slovo*. 02.14.1992.

to take on speedy negotiations on the Central Asian part of the former Sino-Soviet border. This "gentlemen's agreement" represents, of course, some progress when compared to those of yesterday. Nevertheless, it should be remembered that every compromise has two sides: positive and negative. The compromise can bring the final goal much closer, yet simultaneously, can create the dangerous conviction of achieving results which can become illusory under a new political situation. The collapse of the USSR has had a great influence on China. The Chinese regime is going through a process of transformation, while Russia is in uncertainty: to disintegrate, or to built a new authoritarian regime that can broaden Russian "sphere of interests," or to embrace a liberal democracy. The new Central Asian states are strengthening their relations with their Muslim neighbors; some of them are on the edge of civil war. All of these factors can only aggravate the border situation in the region. No agreement really covers the border in the area -- only the status-quo line between the former Soviet (Russian) army, under the formal command of the Commonwealth of Independent States, and Chinese border forces.

It should be stressed that after the collapse of the Soviet Union, China began to look at Russia as a source of ideological instability and a bad influence in the region—even though, the disintegration of the Soviet Union eliminated the military treat from the North. All of this means that China will maintain its forces on the Sino-Russian border and on its borders with Central Asia. At the same time, the reduction of Russian military detachments in the area, the size of the Chinese population, the economic growth of China and the vast underpopulated regions in Siberia and the Russian Far East all indicate that Russia will be still relying on nuclear constraint vis-à-vis China. All of these facts, along with the civil war in Tajikistan in which Afghanistan is also heavily involved, are contributing to destabilization of the region. Another question is to what extent the nuclear factor can play a constraining role in the region, where so many different ethnic communities are struggling to settle the borders that were never settled in the past through peaceful negotiations?

Fortunately, the experience of recent history has convinced Russia and China (and perhaps will convince the new Central Asian states) that disputes over the historical background of the border areas are not productive in the building of stable interstate relations and will only be detrimental to the fragile political stability of any new regime. The facts which prove the historical ownership of some territories by one state always seem to fall short of convincing the opponent. At present times border security, in its strategic understanding, must be ensured, not by military force, but by the interest of all involved sides in the division of tasks and economic cross-pollination for mutual benefit. Only the fulfillment of such prerequisites could thwart the repeat of the sanguinary facts of recent border history in the region[350].

---

[350] See also my article "Are there Still Clouds on the Border ?" in Russian and its variant in English "Some Border Issues Unsolved". *New Times.* #19. 1991.

CONCLUSION

It is clear that the Sino-Russian border and the Central Asian sector of the former Sino-Soviet border (which still lays in both Russia and China's spheres of interests) should be defined by a special diplomatic document and cannot be wholly dependent upon the character of the political relationship between Russia, China and newly independent Central Asian states. The security of the border in the strategic sense during the present situation should be determined not by military means, as before, but by economic interdependence. The decline of Russia's economic potential has completely altered Russia's strategic attitude toward China and Central Asia. Russian attitudes toward the Chinese version of the history of Sino-Russian relations and even to the historical ownership of some disputed regions will be very reasonable compared to Soviet reactions in the near past. But even a small destabilizing event in Russia or in China can revive Sino-Russian territorial problems, which then can lead to an unprecedented situation in the Far East and in Central Asia. This new situation will be very difficult to handle, and should be analyzed thoroughly because of that. The current situation in the Transcaucasus and Yugoslavia proves that in some countries history cannot be easily ignored, and if ignored will lead to unpredictable consequences.

The normalization of the current Sino-Russian relationship is experiencing some results: The polemics on the history of Sino-Russian relations and most of the debatable questions are now taken out of the sphere of interstate relations. In Russia and China, these issues and the difficulties which arise from them are becoming more or less the object of normal scholarly analysis.

The historiography of borders and of the relationships between neighboring countries always raises sensitive and controversial problems intimately tied to questions of sovereignty and legitimacy. This fact — which this book has concentrated on — has been particularly true for Russian and Chinese historians. Within the past several years, both countries have decisively rejected most of the ideological deformations in their relationship which resulted in years of totalitarian rule. It is obvious, however, that political will alone is not enough to resolve all of the problems created by ideological bias. It is important now to push forward in the rethinking of the mutual history of these two giants.

The historiography in China was always considered within the sphere of state interests. For thousands of years, the writing of history in Chinese society has usually been a process of molding events to serve a political purpose. Chinese history was considered "reliable" only if historians rejected "private" views and maintained "standard" (i.e., official) conceptions. When writing about the relations between the Qing dynasty and other states (including Russia) and when using Chinese sources, every researcher should clearly understand how Qing scholars explained the historical process, and what goals they set for themselves when preparing chronicles or other sources. The comparing of Chinese official and unofficial (dissident) sources (which interpreted the facts differently) when substantiated by Russian archival materials, can reveal the hidden motives and underlying reasons, and simultaneously clear up the principles of editing sources by Chinese official historiography. This is why any researcher who uses Chinese sources when writing on Sino-Russian relations or on the history of the international relations in Central Asia must keep in mind that in Chinese sources historical fact was considered valuable if had an appropriate ideological accent, i.e., if the fact corresponded with the appropriate political idea.

Unfortunately, Chinese scholars of the 1980s and the 1990s do not take into consideration all these metatheoretical (or methodological) approaches, and instead base their research on the official Chinese version written during the Qing period. Usually, Chinese historians maintain the same approach to history that was followed in ancient China. All other sources (Russian as well as Western) are used to prove this standard version, i.e., Chinese scholars take from these sources only the facts which correspond with their conceptions, and either reject as nonreliable or do simply not mention all other facts. This approach makes current Chinese concepts highly ideological.

Simultaneously, a similar phenomenon is true for Russian researchers. Being aware of the metatheoretical weakness of the Chinese sources and in many cases successfully reconstructing the historical facts "trimmed" from official Chinese chronicles, they fail to interpret it correctly ceding to the temptation of explaining all events from the standpoint of Russian imperial interests. Most of these scholars for decades considered both the Russian and Soviet empires' policy as wholly representing Russian national interests. It was only after the collapse of the Soviet Union when Russian researchers began to seriously investigate the problem of Russian national interests and the interests of other nations which were incorporated into the Russian state.

The analysis of the Russian and Chinese historiography of the 1980s reveals two approaches to the history of Sino-Russian relations and the history of the formation of the Sino-Russian border equally presented at certain stages in both countries: The development of neighboring territories and the contacts between the two empires was presented as either an "aggression" or the colonization of "economic territories." These two approaches were considered in China, as well as in Russia, as diametrically opposed to one another. It is obvious today that further intensive research in the field of the history of Sino-Russian relations on the basis of only one of these two interpretations is impossible. The creative potential of these two isolated interpretations has been exhausted. The approach with the most potential today is the non-confrontational one, i.e., the analysis of the problem on the basis of modernisation processes, which stress the analyses within a framework of the interaction between different civilizations, Western and Asian.

An analysis of the trends in the historiography of Russia and China of the 1980s can be ended with the following conclusions:

- The Chinese concept, according to which all different nationalities of modern China were participating in the building of the Chinese nation-state is disputable from the scholarly point of view. The appearance of this concept in China can be explained mostly by political reasons. During the past few years, some Chinese researchers have looked at this concept critically, trying to change or develop some earlier appraisals.

- The Russian side should understand that from the metatheoretical point of view, the Chinese concept of the unequal character of past Sino-Russian relations for China has every right to exist, because it is supported by "experience" (i.e., by some historical facts). It does not mean that this concept cannot be criticized; but at the same time modern social sciences cannot be developed without taking the Chinese point of view into consideration.

- Chinese research in the 1980s elaborated upon the traditional Chinese concept of Sino-Russian relations. Nevertheless some key points of this concept were modernized in late 1980s, marking a considerable conceptual shift compared to the 1960s and 1970s. According to this modernized concept, there is a well-defined line separating the policies of the Tsarist and Soviet Russia toward China. The fall of the Communist government in Russia has resulted in the designation of practically all interesting works on this subject in China, but it is obvious that Chinese social sciences are on the threshold of a new conceptual shift in the research of Russian studies. This shift is dependent completely on the political situation in China and the struggle for power within the Communist circles.

  Analysts in the former Soviet Union have made a clear mistake: The Chinese ideas of the "aggressive character" of Tsarist Russia's policy toward China in the late 1980s have primarily internal reasons for emergence. These concepts should be explained mostly by the necessity for strengthening the Chinese state and providing a legitimate base for reforming the economy. But any further political destabilization in China or in Russia can easily revive the territorial disputes especially in the Central Asian part of the post-Soviet territories and make use of these concepts.

- The positions of Russian and Chinese researchers concerning the history of Sino-Soviet relations in the past few years were diametrically opposed. According to some Russian historians, the initial premise of Chinese scholars is not correct: the Russian state is shown as the only permanent active subject of history. For Chinese researchers, even the economic aspects of Russian activity in the Far East and Central Asia are considered as "the expansion of Russian Tsarism," and they do not consider any external historical forces, mistakenly identify national and state interests, etc. Simultaneously, the Chinese perception of the history of Sino-Russian relations should be thoroughly analyzed since this analysis can aid in the correction of former Soviet simplistic concepts, especially concerning the character of interstate relations within the Russian sphere of interests.

Conclusion

- The evolution of Russian and Chinese historiography on the theme marks a new stage of research in the field. The parameters of this new stage can be defined by the incorporation of a variety of primary sources, and different, or maybe even controversial, concepts with serious attention to the contiguous historical and cultural problems into the balanced interpretation of relations between the two states. The basis for this new stage of studies could be the concept advocating the proximity of Russian and Chinese basic interests, and the differences or even the juxtaposition of their state (imperial) interests during concrete historical periods. The approaches to these concepts are theoretically outlined in works by a few Russian and Chinese scholars, but still are clearly dependent upon the political situation in both countries.

CONCISE CHRONOLOGY OF RUSSIAN-CHINESE RELATIONS

1618	The first diplomatic contact between the Russian state with the Chinese Empire of Ming: Ivan Petlin and his comrades travel to China and open a way to Peking via Siberia and Mongolia.
1618	Edict by the Ming Emperor Wanli allowing Russians to send missions and to trade in China.
1654-1658	F. Baikov's mission - the first official Russian mission to China.
1675-1677	N.G. Spafari's mission to China.
1686-1690	F.A. Golovin's mission to China for the demarcation of the border between the Russian and Chinese domains in the Far East.
August 27, 1689[351]	Russian-Chinese Peace Treaty of Nerchinsk on borders and trade conditions - the first treaty between Qing China and a foreign state.
December 1689	Beginning of regular caravan trade with China.
1692-1695	Ye.I. Ides' mission to China for trade negotiations.
1698	Beginning of interstate trade with China.

[351] The dates before 1918 are cited by the Russian old-style calendar.

1714	Arrival of the first Chinese mission by Tulishen within Russian domains.
1716-1718	L. Lang's -- the first Russian trade agent -- stay in China.
1716	Establishment of the Russian Orthodox Church mission in China.
1719-1722	L. Izmailov's mission to China for signing a trade agreement.
1724-1728	S.L. Vladislavich-Raguzinskyi's mission to China in order "to restore and assert the former, favorable agreement and the freedom of trade."
August 20, 1727	Signing of the Treaty of Burinsk on border demarcation between Russia and China.
October 21, 1727	Signing of the Treaty of Kyakhta, containing the provisions for political and economic relations between Russia and China and claiming that "the new treaty is realized especially in order to bring about a solid and eternal peace between the two Empires" (Article 1).
1728	First Chinese and Manchu books appear in Russia; brought by L. Lang from Peking, those books started the Chinese and Manchu library collections of the Russian Academy of Science.
1731-1732	Chinese mission to Russia.
1735	Russian Academy of Sciences provided L. Lang with its publications and authorized him to sell or exchange these in China.
1737	Manchu language courses, taught by Zhou Ge (Fyodor Dzhoga) were opened at the Moscow office of the Collegium for Foreign Affairs.

1756	K. Bratishchev's mission to China.
1762	Opening of the Chinese and Manchu language school in St.Petersburg.
August 7, 1762	Tsar's edict of awarding Al. Leontiev and I.K. Rossokhin for their translation of "Detailed Description of the Origin and the State of the Manchu People and the Army of the Eight Banners" (16 volumes).
1768	I. Kropotov's mission to China.
February 8, 1792	Signing of the act which prescribed the rules for Russian-Chinese trade via Kyakhta.
1805	Yu.A. Golovkin's mission to China.
1805	I.F. Kruzenshtern's and Yu.A. Lisyanskyi's global expedition visits Guanzhou.
1819	First publication of the Chinese lithograph texts in St.Petersburg.
1830	Opening of the Chinese language school in Kyakhta.
1837	Opening of the Chair for the Chinese language at the Oriental Department at Kazan University.
April 12, 1841	Edict by Nicholas I prohibiting Russian merchants of trading opium in China.
1844	Opening of the Chair for the Manchu language in Kazan University.
1845	The Russian Academy of Sciences donated 357 books on Russian history and geography, as well as books written by Russian scholars and scientists on mathematics, pharmacology, gardening, literature, and other disciplines, to the Qing government.

July 25, 1851	Signing of the Russian-Chinese Treaty on trade in Kulja and Chuguchak, by which "this trade treaty, signed for the benefit of both states and witnessing the care taken for peace and welfare of their respective citizens, shall consolidate an even stronger mutual friendship between the two powers" (Article 1).
November 1853	I.A. Goncharov, a renown Russian writer, visits Shanghai on the frigate "Pallada."
October 22, 1854	Opening of the Chair for the Chinese and Manchu languages at St.Petersburg University.
May 16, 1858	Signing of the Treaty of Aigun on the Far Eastern border between the two states and on Russian-Chinese trade in Amuria "... for mutual friendship between the citizens of the two states" (Article 2).
June 1, 1858	Signing of the Treaty of Tientsin on a framework for political relations between Russia and China.
November 2, 1860	Signing of the Corollary Treaty of Peking defining the Russian-Chinese borders, the order of diplomatic relations, and trade in Kulja, "for the better consolidation of the mutual friendship between the two Empires, the development of trade relations and the prevention of misunderstanding" (Preamble).
1861	Establishment of a permanent Russian diplomatic mission in Peking.
1861-1862	Military training of Chinese soldiers and officers by Russian instructors, provided within the framework of Russian assistance to China.
February 20, 1862	Signing of "experimental" Regulations for Mainland Trade between Russia and China.

1862	Opening of the Tongwenguan - the school of foreign languages, run by the Chinese Ministry of Foreign Affairs for teaching, in particular, the Russian language on the foundation of the Russian school for translators which existed in the early 18th century.
September 25, 1864	Signing of the Chuguchak Protocol of the Russian-Chinese border demarcation.
July 1, 1866	Order of the Russian government prohibiting Russian citizens from enrolling and bringing in the Chinese "koolee" (carriers).
April 15, 1869	Signing of the Regulations for Mainland Trade between Russia and China.
February 12, 1881	Signing of the Russian-Chinese Treaty of St. Petersburg (The Ili Treaty) on the return of the Ili Valley to China and on trade in Western China.
February 12, 1881	Signing of the Regulations for Mainland Trade between Russia and China adopted in compliancy with the Treaty of St.Petersburg.
1884	The Russian Senate's edict on the opening of the school for translators of the Chinese, Manchu, and Mongolian languages in Urga and Kulja.
February 8, 1884	Gui Rong, an official of the Chinese Embassy in Russia, was approved as a freelance teacher of conversational Chinese and of Chinese calligraphy.
August 13, 1892	Signing of the telegraph convention between Russia and China.
April 23, 1895	Protest by Russia, France, and Germany against the annexation of the Liaodong Peninsula by Japan.

June 24, 1895	The Russian-Chinese Declaration of a loan to China.
May 22, 1896	The Treaty of Alliance between Russia and China mutually agreed by "the Chinese Emperor and... the Russian Emperor willing to take advantage of their relations of peace... and to protect the Asian continent against any new foreign intervention" (Preamble).
August 27, 1896	Signing of the contract between the Russian and Chinese governments on the building and exploitation of the Chinese Eastern Railway.
1897	Publication of the treatise by Yan Fu, a prominent Chinese thinker, "On China's Friendship with Russia."
August 1897 -1901	Construction of the Chinese Eastern Railway.
March 15, 1898	Signing of the Russian-Chinese Convention on the leasing of Port-Arthur and Dalian (Dairen) to Russia.
1899	Opening of the Oriental Institute in Vladivostok.
1909	Opening of the Practical Oriental Academy — Chinese and Japanese language courses — in St.Petersburg.
April 27, 1909	Preliminary Russian-Chinese Agreement on the order of administration in the "alienation belt" of the Chinese Eastern Railway, by which "as a main principle, the supreme rights of China shall be recognized and must not be infringed upon in any way" (Article 1).
October 23, 1913	Signing of the Russian Declaration recognizing the autonomy of Outer Mongolia.

Concise Chronology of Russian-Chinese Relations 115

May 25, 1915	Signing of the Russian-Chinese-Mongolian trilateral Agreement on the autonomy of Outer Mongolia.
July 25, 1919	The Address by the RSFSR Soviet of Peoples' Commissars to the Chinese people and the governments of Southern and Northern China announcing the repudiation of all privileges forcefully gained by Tsarism from China.
1917 - 1991	The period of Sino-Soviet relations.
December 1992	The visit of Boris Yeltsin, first Russian President, to China.
December 19, 1992	The publication of the Joint Declaration on the basic relationship between The People's Republic of China and the Russian Federation.

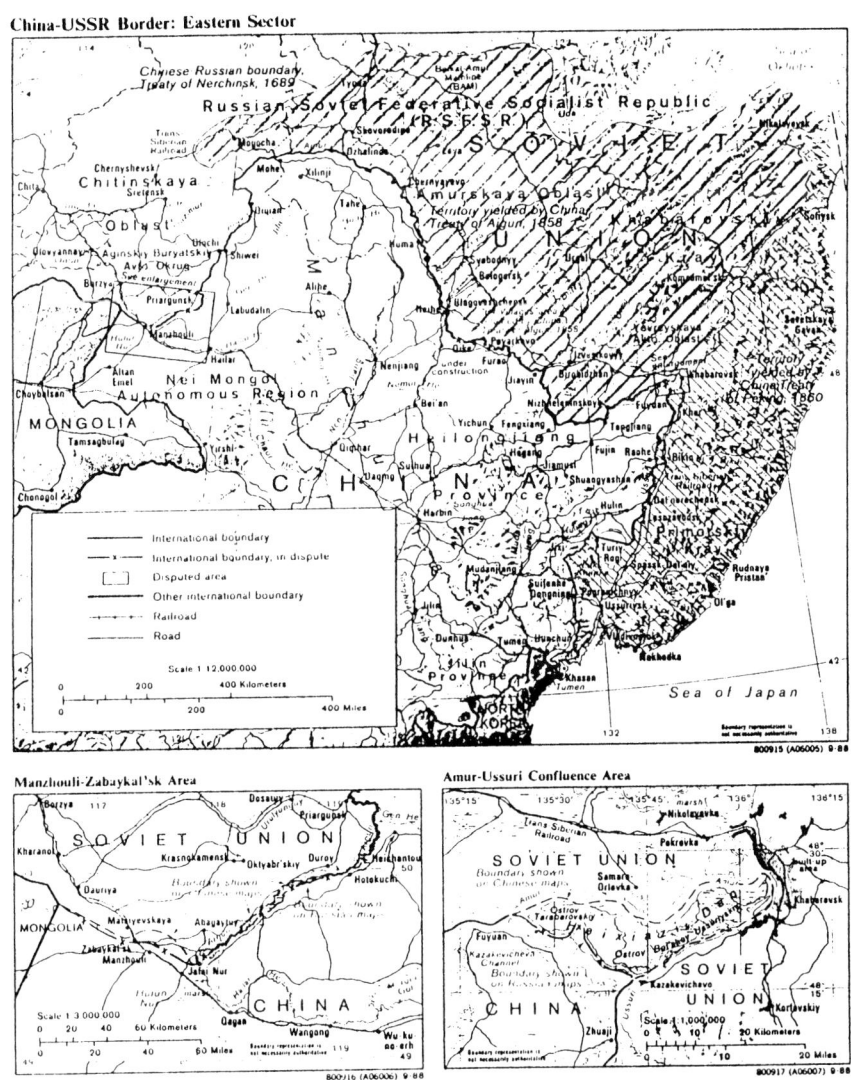

China- USSR Boundary, US Department of State, Washington D.C., 13 February 1978, International Boundary Study

China-USSR Border

800913 (A06003) 9-86

China-USSR Border: Western Sector

800914 (A06004) 9-86

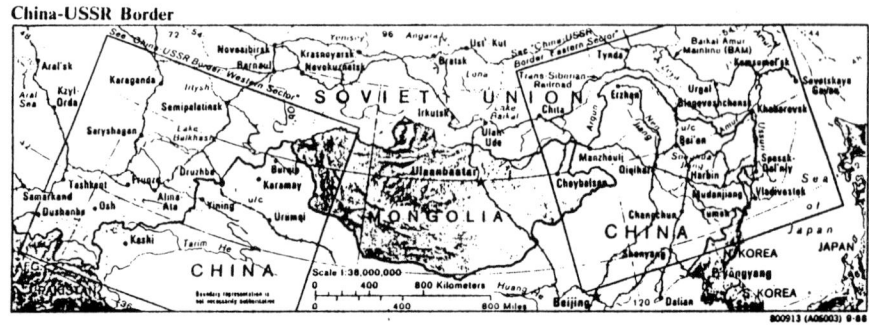

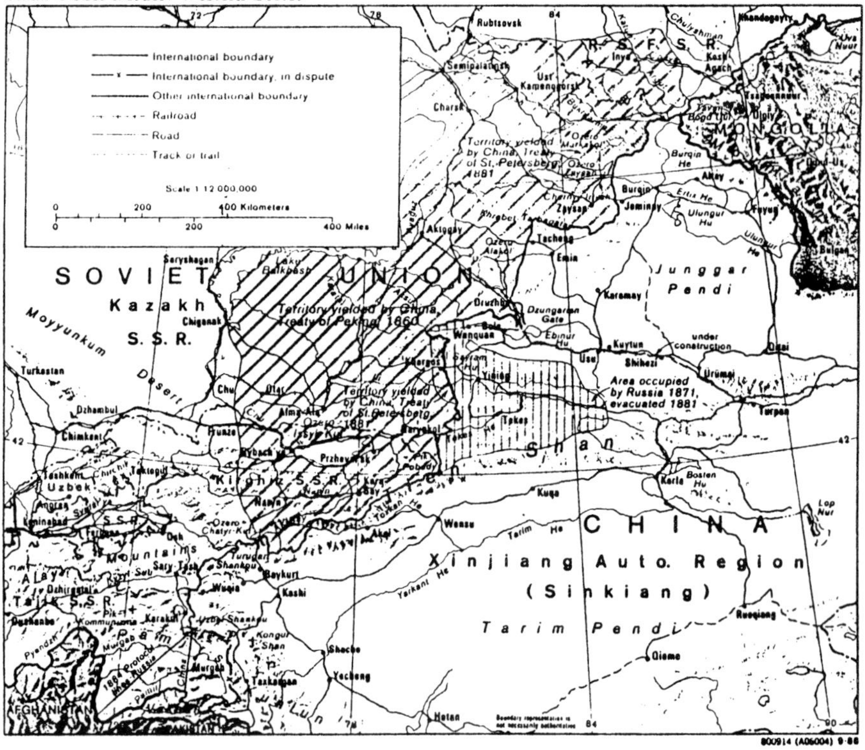

沙俄割占中国领土示意图:
①沙俄通过1858年中俄《瑷珲条约》割去黑龙江以北外兴安岭以南60多万平方公里的中国领土。②沙俄通过1860年中俄《北京条约》割去乌苏里江以东约40万平方公里的中国领土。③1858年中俄《瑷珲条约》规定，江东六十四屯地区中国人有永久居住权，中国政府有永久管辖权。④沙俄通过1860年中俄《北京条约》和1864年中俄《勘分西北界约记》割去44万多平方公里的中国领土。⑤沙俄通过1881年中俄《改订条约》和以后5个勘界议定书割去7万多平方公里的中国领土。⑥1884年中俄《续勘喀什噶尔界约》规定自乌孜别里山口起"俄国界线转向西南，中国界线一直往南。"⑦沙俄通过1911年中俄《满洲里界约》割去中国的领土。

The territorial acquisitions of Russia in China in the 19 Century

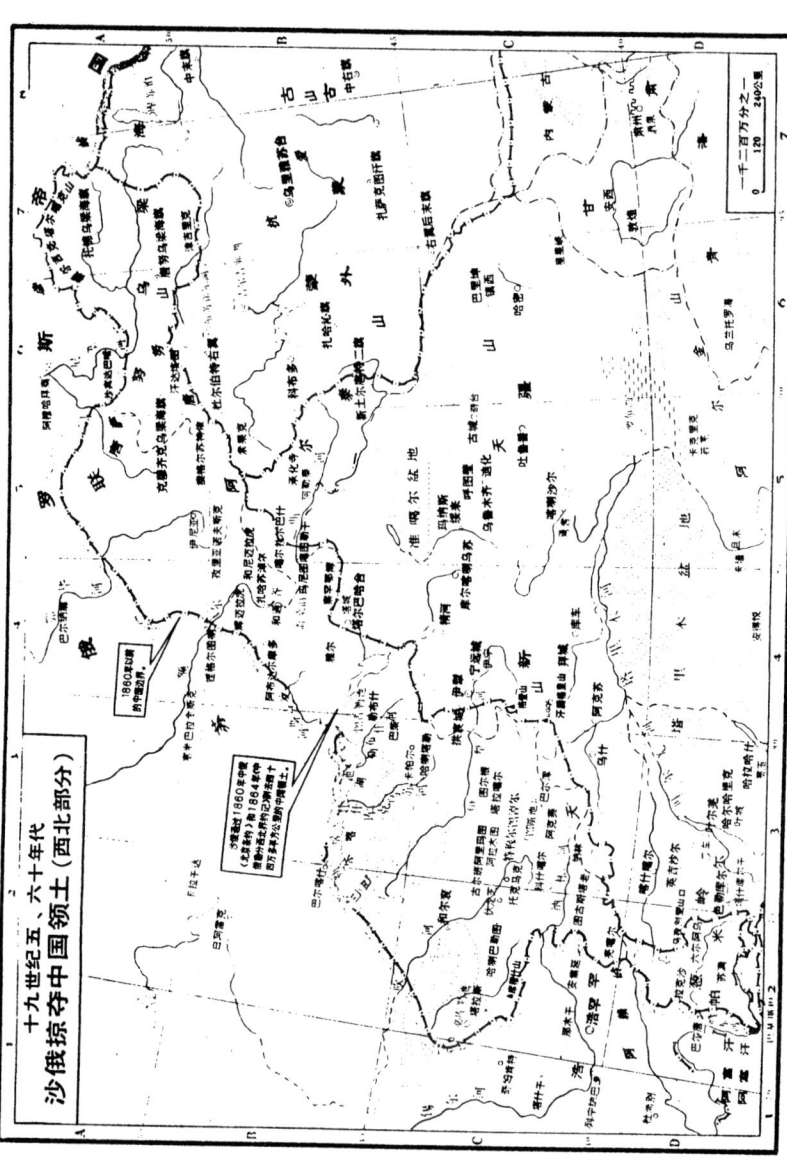

The territorial acquisitions of Russia on the Western Sector of the Sino-Russian border in the 19th Century

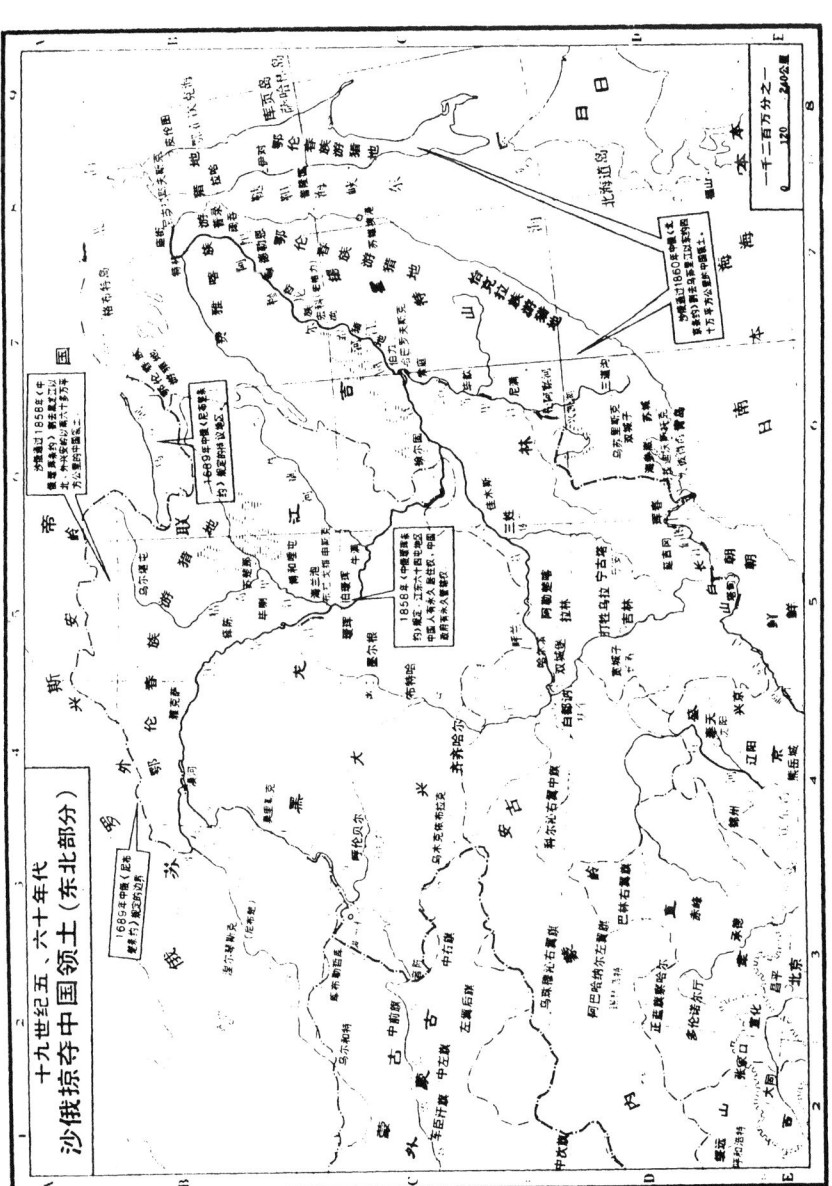

The territorial acquisitions of Russia on the Eastern Sector of the Sino-Russian border in the 19th Century

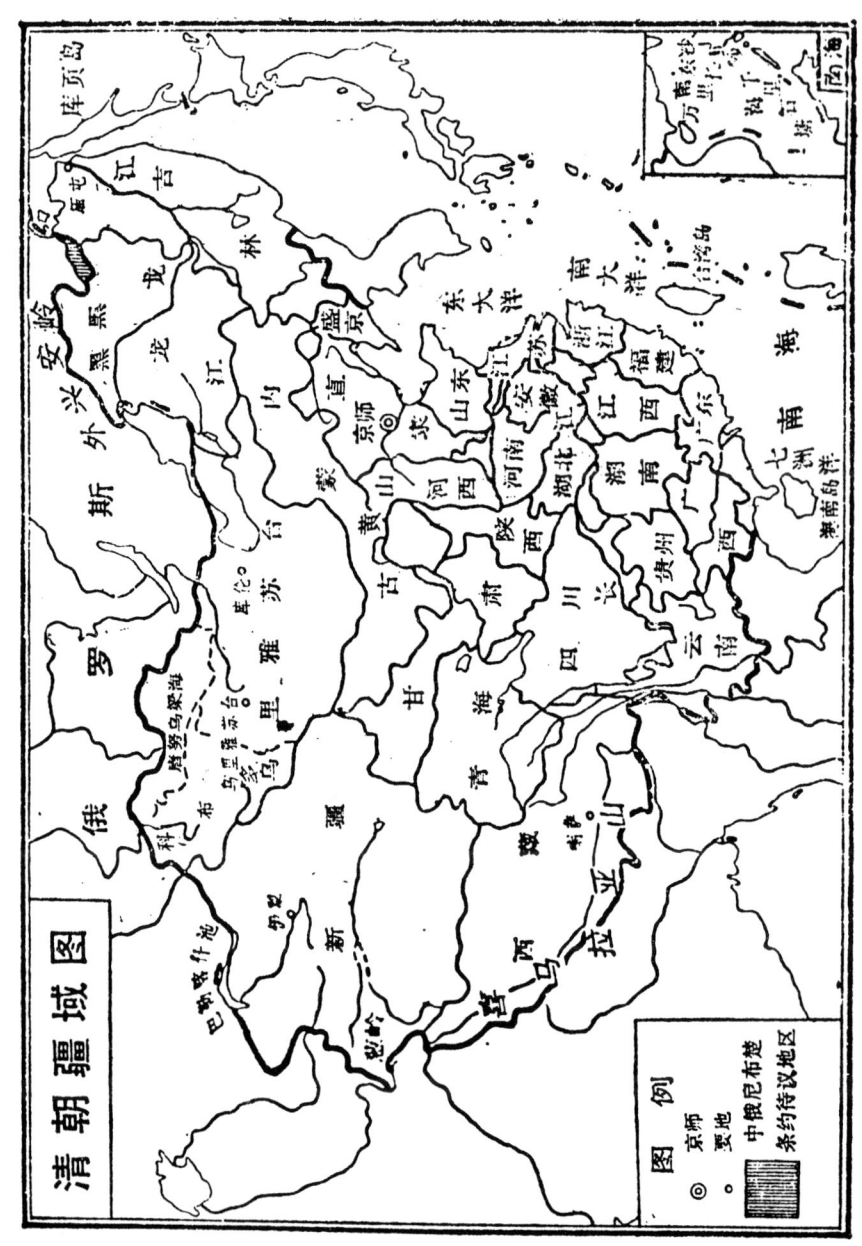

SUBJECT INDEX

—A—

A Joint Communique, 96
Aigun Treaty, 78
Ainu, 35
Aksu River, 38
Amur River, 64, 78
Amur) River, 61
Argun River, 73, 94
Asian-Pacific theater, 97
Attitudes Toward Imperial Russia, 27

—B—

Barga, 59
Bole, 38
border problems, 23
border violations, 90
Boris Yeltsin, 115
Boxer Uprising, 83
Boyar Golovin, 73
Bratishchev's mission to China, 110
Bureau or Committee of Historiography (*Goushiguan*), 16

—C—

Capitalism in Russia, 71
caravan trade, 109
Center for China's Borderland History, 8
Central Asia, 36, 74, 88
Central Asian states, 101
Central Asian) sector, 42
Chinese Academy of Social Sciences, 8
Chinese Conceptions of Sino-Russian, 23
Chinese Eastern Railway, 114
Chouban Yiwu Shimo, 18
Chronicle of, 109
Chronicles (Qing Shilu), 15
Chuguchak Protocol, 113
classification, 14
Communist Party of China, 91
Communist Party of the Soviet Union, 91
Corollary Treaty of Peking, 79, 112
Cossacks, 41

—D—

Dalian, 114
Dongbei, 35
Dzungars, 30

—E—

Eastern Sector, 41
eastern sector of the border, 94
eastern sector of the former Sino-Soviet border, 99
economy, 75

—F—

F. Baikov's mission, 109
Far East theater, 98

Foreign policy, 75
forest fires, 90

—G—

General Buyantai, 37
Golovin's mission to China, 109
Golovkin's mission to China, 111
Greater Sayany Range, 75
gshi (The Qing History), 19
Guomindang period, 7

—H—

Hailongjiang [Amur] River Basin, 42
Heilongjiang and Ussuri Rivers, 54
Heilongjiang region, 27

—I—

Ides' mission to China, 109
Ili Valley, 38, 49, 80, 113
imperial chronicles, 13
Imperial Russia, 27
Irtish River, 37
Islamic fundamentalism, 88

—J—

Japan, 59
Japanese militarism, 57

—K—

Karatal River, 38
Kazakhs, 31
Kazakhstan, 30, 76
khanates, 31
Kropotov's mission to China, 111
Kyakhta, 80
Kyrgyz nationality, 33

—L—

L. Izmailov's mission to China, 110
Lake Baikal, 50
Lake Balkhash, 37
Lake Khanka, 94

laws of interaction, 81
Lena River, 42, 50

—M—

Main Directorate of Foreign Affairs (*Zongliyamen*), 19
Manchu population, 78
Manchuria, 57, 58
metatheoretical approach, 14
military forces, 97
Mongolia, 44, 52
Mongolian dynasty of Yuan, 70

—N—

National Histories, 28
national interests, 76
navigability of the border rivers, 89
northeastern China, 57
northern border regions, 36
Northern territories, 99
northwestern [sic] regions of China, 36

—O—

official or standard histories, 13
Opium War, 37
Oriental Institute in Vladivostok, 114
Outer Mongolia, 52, 58, 59, 63, 114, 115

—P—

Pamir, 33, 51
Pamirs, 81
Peter the Great, 47
Port-Arthur, 114
Practical Oriental Academy, 114

—Q—

Qier, 38
Qing dynasty, 7
Qing Empire, 72, 76
Qing period, 13, 15

Qing Shilu, 16
Qingji Waijiao Shiliao, 18, 19
Qingshi Gao (The Draft History of the Qing Dynasty), 19

—R—

Regulations for Mainland Trade, 113
Revolution of 1917 in Russia, 83
Russian foreign policy in the 18th century, 43
Russian foreign policy toward China, 47
Russian Orthodox Church, 110
Russian-Chinese Declaration of a loan to China, 114
Russian-Chinese trade via Kyakhta, 111
Russian-Chinese Treaty Acts, 70
Russian-Chinese Treaty of St. Petersburg, 113
Russian-Chinese Treaty on trade in Kulja and Chuguchak, 112
Russo-Chinese border formation in Central Asia, 51
Russo-Japanese War, 56

—S—

Sakhalin, 34
Sarykol Range, 81
Second Opium War, 46
Semirechie area, 38
Shabin-Dabaga Pass, 75
Shandong province, 60
Shilka River, 73
Shilu, 15
Siberia, 51, 70
Siberian line of fortification, 37
Sino-British Corollary Agreement, 79
Sino-British Nanking Treaty, 79
Sino-Russian Treaty of 1896, 57
Sino-Russian Treaty of Ili, 48
Sino-Russian Treaty of Livadia, 48
Sino-Soviet border, 88, 100

Soviet-Chinese Negotiations on the Settlement of Border Questions, 92
Spafari's mission to China, 109
St. Petersburg (or Ili) Treaty, 80
St. Petersburg treaty, 32
state interests, 76
statehood in China, 56
systematization of Chinese primary sources, 13

—T—

Tannu-Uryanhai, 59
Tibet, 52
Tientsin Treaty, 77
timber industry, 89
trade, 53, 74
trade relations, 74
trading opium in China, 111
Treaty of Aigun, 45, 78, 112
Treaty of Burinsk, 45, 75, 110
Treaty of Commerce, 44
Treaty of Friendship, Union and Mutual Assistance, 88
Treaty of Ili, 53
Treaty of Kyakhta, 75, 110
Treaty of Nanking, 44
Treaty of Nerchinsk, 41, 45, 51, 54, 64, 73, 109
Treaty of Peking, 32, 79, 80
Treaty of St. Petersburg, 81
Treaty of Tientsin, 79, 112

—U—

unofficial (dissident) histories, 14
Urga, 80
Ussuri River, 34, 64, 95
Ussuri Territory, 79

—V—

Vernyi, 38
Vladislavich-Raguzinskyi's mission to China, 110

—X—

Xinjiang, 53

—Y—

Yangtze River basin, 57
Yihetuan rebellion, 83

—Z—

Zheltorossia, 59
Ziang Zeming, 98

Augsburg College
George Sverdrup Library
Minneapolis, MN 55454